What Reader's are Saying About *"Journey to the Father"*

This collection of endearing stories is both heartwarming and inspiring. You'll be drawn into the arms of your Heavenly Father!

—*Bob Sorge, Author of Secrets of the Secret Place, Bobsorge.com*

The story of salvation and new life in Christ is a divine journey, initiated by a Heavenly Father who pursued us with reckless abandon. It is this unreasonable love that changes us and sets in motion a lifelong pilgrimage towards the center of the heart of God for every child of God. In *Journey to the Father*, Sonny and Becky Misar wisely roll out the topographical map for this journey and guide us forward. This message is greatly needed in our day when so many are hungering to go places in God that exist below the surface and beyond our previous borders of experience. I am personally grateful for these messengers and the prophetic message that they bring to the Body of Christ.

—*Lee Cummings, Senior Leader of Radiant Church, Radiant Network, Author of Be Radiant*

Building on the spiritual strength and practical illustrations of their first book, Sonny and Becky beautifully share wonderful stories that lead the reader to experience the Father heart of God. The Biblical insights were mined from deep knowledge of the Scriptures. You will laugh, cry and most importantly, seek to apply the principles found in this book. I've seen them live out these principles firsthand for over 20 years. You'll be glad they're sharing them with you!

—*Pastor Rick Iglesias, Executive Pastor, Orchard Hill Church, Wexford, PA*

Many men and women are deeply wounded because of the absence, abandonment or abuse of an earthly father. Written in a highly transparent fashion, *Journey to the Father* recognizes that uncovering a wound is not enough, for an uncovered yet uncleansed injury forms a scab and emotional scabs can impede the healing process. Journey to the Father targets one of life's deepest hurts and offers practical steps that result in hearing from the Father, "This is my beloved child, with who I am well pleased."

—*Dr. Bill Effler, Associate Professor of Pastoral Studies, Lee University, Author of Out From the Shadows, Biblical Counseling Revealed in the Story of Creation*

Journey to the Father may be used as a powerful healing tool to bring about restoration of relationship between one's natural father and one's Heavenly Father. Many other areas of healing are possible as these insightful teachings mixed with inspiring life stories ministers to the deficits in one's soul.

—*Dr. Shirley Harvey, Teacher and co-founder of Covenant Life Ministries, Clyde, NC*

Sonny and Becky's book is well written, provides excellent examples from Becky's childhood experiences with her own earthly father and is well packed with relevant Scriptures. This book can help the reader feel confidence and motivation to take needed steps toward healing his or her "father wound".

—*Teresa Koehler, International Storyteller, King's Commission Ministries, Inc*

Every human heart is attracted to a place where peace, contentment, intimacy and encouragement prevail, a place with no pre-conditions or pretense. Finding this 'place'— which is more condition than location— is a lifelong search for many but describes both the journey and destination for most Christ-followers. Sonny and Becky Misar's latest work, *Journey to the Father*, illustrates with great accuracy and simplicity the nature of life lived in such a place. Through a series of personal stories, the Father's heart is revealed as both a destination and a journey and is described in insightful ways that most readers will find illuminating. I commend Journey to the Father in the knowledge that its contents are simultaneously profound and simple— an ideal vehicle for truth.

—*Timothy W. Jack, National Leader, Apostolic Church United Kingdom*

God has called us not just to believe in creeds and recite them faithfully, but He has called us into a real relationship with Himself. Our wealth or poverty as Christians is defined by how we understand and handle this relationship. In *Journey to the Father*, Sonny and Becky draw from Becky's relationship with her father to paint powerful pictures of God that will help every Christian on this journey of discovery. This is worth any investment of time and resources; go for it!

—*Dr. Aaron Nartey Ami-Narh, MD, Sr. Pastor, District Five Apostolic Church, Ghana, Africa*

We live in a world where the majority of people think of God as being all-powerful and all knowing, but distant and unapproachable. In *Journey to the Father* the true nature of God the Father is beautifully revealed through the eyes of a daughter reflecting on her loving earthly father. Our Heavenly Father is deeply in love with His children, enjoys having us around and proudly watches on as we develop into maturity, representing His heart and character.

—*Dale E Hewitt, Apostolic Leader, Dreambuilders Network of Churches, Perth, Australia*

Journey to the Father, Copyright © 2017 by R. Sonny Misar.

Printed in the United States of America

ISBN: 978-0-9886583-5-6

Cover, interior design, and composition by Laurie Nelson, Agápe Design Studios, Winona, MN 55987, www.agapedesignstudios.com

Photos: © iStockphoto.com

All scripture quotations, unless otherwise indicated, are taken from the Holy Bible, New International Version®, NIV®. Copyright ©1973, 1978, 1984 by Biblica, Inc.™ Used by permission of Zondervan. All rights reserved worldwide. www.zondervan.com

Italics or bold within Scripture quotations reflect the author's added emphasis.

All rights reserved. No part of this book may be reproduced or transmitted in any form or by any means, electronic or mechanical, including photocopying and recording, or by any information storage and retrieval system, without permission in writing from the author.

Published by

AGÁPE STUDIOS

Agápe Studios, Winona, MN 55987

Acknowledgments

Our deep appreciation goes out to the many people who encouraged us and helped bring this project to life. We wish to thank Juliette Misar, Sonny's mom, for preparing a gracious space for us to get away and write most of this manuscript. Thanks to Paul and Denise Grafenberg who also opened their lovely Florida condo which helped us break through writer's block. We are grateful to our editing team: Katie Abbot, Rev. Paul and Dianne Midgett and Diana Flegal of Hartline Literary Agency. Much thanks to our friend, Laurie Nelson at Agápe Design Studios for her outstanding graphic work and for entering into this project heart and soul. Heaven only knows how many people backed us in prayer throughout the writing process...thank you hidden warriors! Mostly, we thank our Lord who continually makes Himself known to us as a good and loving Father. All glory belongs to Him.

Dedication

In honor of Becky's dad, Denver Jones— a husband, father, pastor, and patriarch of a "delightful inheritance" in the land of his calling.

Journey to the Father

Discovering God's Lavish Love for You

R. Sonny & Becky Misar

Introduction 11

1 **"Our Father"** 21

2 **Father's Identity** – *"My Daddy calls me Love"* 31

3 **Father's Acceptance** –
  "Horsey Rides in the Holy of Holies" 41

4 **Father's Care** – *"The Saving Qualities of Tea"* 51

5 **Father's Delight** - *"Front and Center"* 63

6 **Father's Kindness** – *"Jesus Goes to Jail"* 73

7 **Father's Discipline** – *"The Chicken Coop Confession"* . . . 81

8 **Father's Presence** – *"Pillar of Hope"* 91

9 **Father's Provision** – *"Gifts Unforeseen"* 101

10 **Father's Comfort** – *"The Family Nest"* 111

11 **Father's Praise** – *"Mourning into Dancing"* 121

12 **Father's Grace** - *"Father's Day Foibles"* 131

Contents

13 Father's Will – *"Monkey See, Monkey Want"*. 141

14 Father's Compassion – *"The Power of a Peanut"* 151

15 Father's Patience - *"You're a Good Kid"* 163

16 Father's Forgiveness – *"Offense-Free Living"*. 173

17 Father's Love – *"Perfect Love Drives out Fear"* 185

18 Father's Favor – *"A Diamond from Heaven"* 195

19 Healing Your Father Wound 205

Appendix A
"A Mighty Oak has Fallen in the Woods Today". 216

Appendix B
"Because of You, Dad" 218

Appendix C
A Father's Prayer. 220

Appendix D
Biblical Attributes of Your Heavenly Father. 222

Credits 225

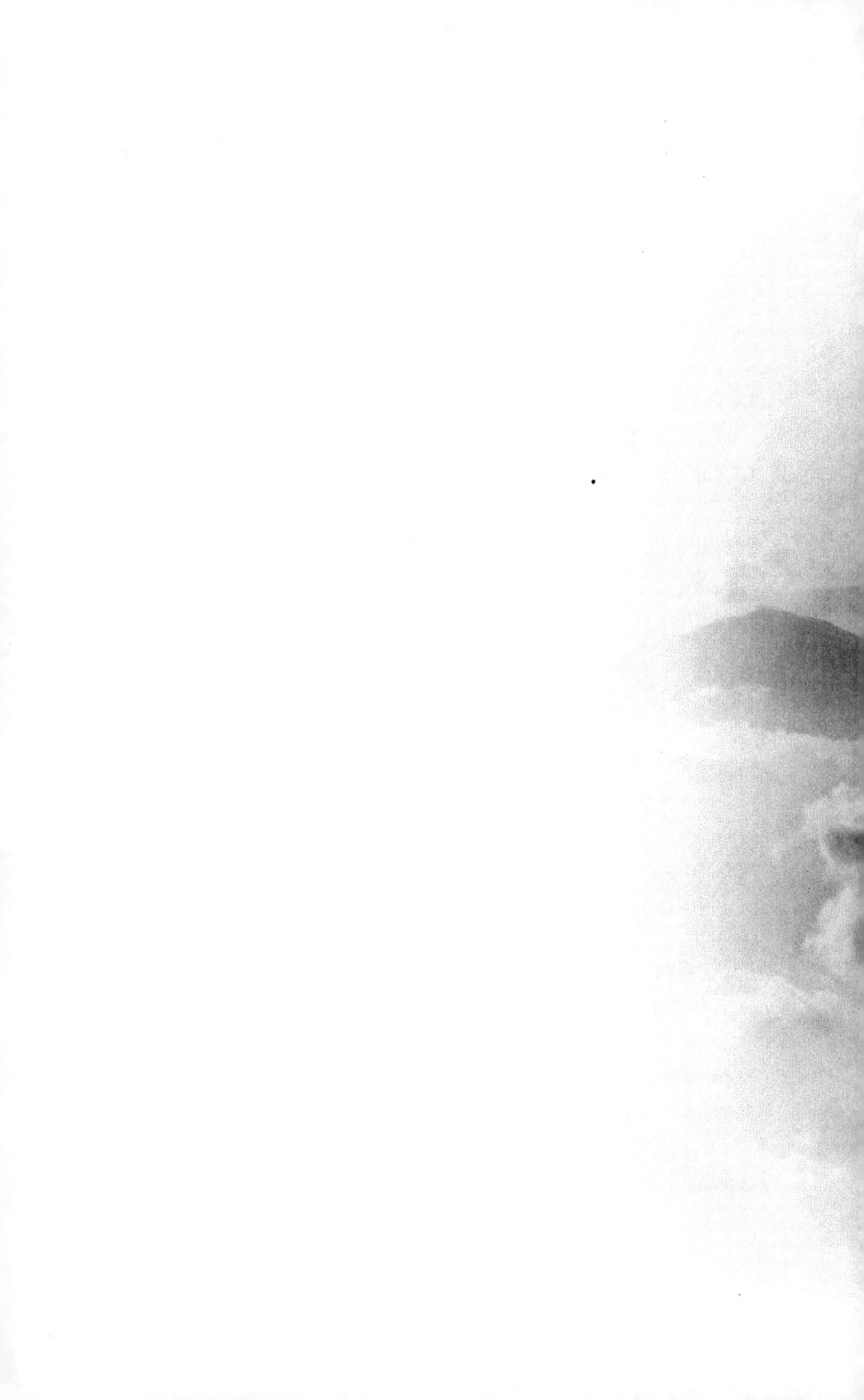

Our Father in Heaven

Introduction

Our Father in heaven: pause for a moment and ponder these words. Better yet, make them personal, "*my* Father in heaven". Let that phrase simmer in your mind for a while until it finds its way to your heart. What is our Heavenly Father like? What does He mean to you personally, and why does it matter? The exploration of these simple, yet profound questions forms the essence of this book.

The term "father" evokes a myriad of thoughts and feelings in us. We may remember a nurturing, affirming, protecting father. Others of us are drawn back to painful memories of harshness, rejection, and abandonment. If we asked a thousand people to describe their relationship with their father, we would likely get a thousand different answers. Yet, as Christians, we are asked to see God as our Father. This can be positive or problematic depending on whether or not our earthy fathers reflected God's character and nature. To varying degrees, our perception of God as our Father is most certainly affected by our relationship with our earthy fathers.

Our spiritual life is only as rich, satisfying, and effective as our concept of God. Pastor and author, A. W. Tozer in his book *The Knowledge of the Holy* asserts, "What comes into our minds when we think about God is the most important thing about us." Yet, many Christians today live with a damaged or distorted view of God as their loving Heavenly Father. This subtle condition robs them of the true joy, confidence, and intimacy purchased for them by Christ Jesus. Take in this powerful revelation penned by John, the beloved disciple, *"How great is the love the Father has lavished on us, that we should be called children of God! And that is what we are"* (1 John 3:1). If we are to walk in all that God has for us, this central truth must lie as the bedrock of our faith: God is our loving Father.

God is pleased to make Himself known to anyone who will receive Him. He took divine initiative, making the first move in opening the door to relationship; *"While we were still sinners, Christ died for us"* (Romans 5:8). Though He is relentless in His pursuit of us, relationship with Him requires a human response. This is His promise: Draw near to Him, and He will draw near to you (James 4:8). With this promise, He breaks all the rules of fairness with His generosity. We "baby step" toward Him, and He "giant steps" toward us.

Through this book you will be introduced to stories of Becky's relationship with her dad, Denver Jones. These "parables" powerfully illustrate what God is like as our Father. Though Denver was not a perfect dad, he was a godly man who loved his children well. Before we go any further, let us introduce you to Denver Jones. His life glorified God and will give context to the "father stories" you are about to read.

Introduction

Denver Jones (1919-2004)
Rags to Riches

"Denver Jones Rags and Bones," was a name given to Denver by some of the children in the small coal-mining village of Tonyrefail, South Wales, where he was born and raised. The description was fitting in many respects: poor, skinny coal miner's kid from nowhere, going no place special. When asked as a child by the school headmaster what he wanted to be when he grew up, he had an immediate response, "A coal miner, sir." This was the grandest vision he could see for himself. That all began to change in 1935 when at age 16, he opened his heart to Christ.

This came about in a surprising way. A massive tent had been erected in an open field outside of his village where evangelistic meetings would be held for several weeks. The spiritual fires were still smoldering from The Great Welsh Revival, which set the country of Wales ablaze in 1904-1906. Denver, always full of mischief, along with two other curious boys, slid in the back door of the tent one night with intentions of making fun of what was going on. Their antics were halted not long into the meeting when an usher, kindly but firmly, told them they needed to either straighten up or leave the premises. Denver found himself moving to a seat closer to the front while the other boys bolted out the back door. Denver could not recall the message preached that night, but he responded to the salvation invitation at the close of the service. In that moment of surrender, his life was forever changed. He quickly made his way home to share the news of his new found faith. Denver was the first in his family of nine kids to become a Christian. He was also the family comedian. Consequently, when He burst through the door and joyfully exclaimed, "I've been saved," they laughed

Journey to the Father

at what sounded like his latest joke. Without any further explanation, he went straight to his bedroom, got on his knees and prayed. In those moments, God gave him assurance of his salvation. The fruit of that decision remained, and the result was that many others in his family would also come to know Christ.

The early years of Denver's Christian experience were characterized by an insatiable hunger to know God. He embraced the daily disciplines of diligent study of the Scripture and prayer, establishing patterns that remained constant throughout his lifetime. The leaders of his church took him under their wing, helping him grow and, challenging him to develop and use his God-given gifts. Ministry to children was one way God used him in those early years. While Denver made his living as a coal miner from ages 14 to 34, God was preparing him for something else: to be a church-planting pastor. "From coal pit to pulpit," as Denver would say.

A pivotal and clarifying time in his life came in 1954 when a Scottish Evangelist, John Pridie, asked if Denver would accompany him on a ministry trip to the USA. Setting sail on the *Queen Elizabeth I*, and no sooner having left the shores of his beloved homeland, God spoke 3 specific things to his heart: "You will never return to live in Wales again, you will find your wife in America, and I will give you a great inheritance in that land." I wonder what Denver Jones Rags and Bones thought of that?

Denver was 35 years old at this time and longed to be married. He always said, "I searched Scotland, Ireland, England, and Wales for a wife. Each time I thought I'd found 'Ms. Right.' God would say, 'wrong'." His hopes of finding a wife now renewed, the ship couldn't sail fast enough! They landed in New York Harbor and immediately made the journey to their first ministry destination: Church of the New Covenant in Minneapolis, Minnesota. Denver's words best tell the rest of the story regarding his search for "Ms. Right": "The first church we visited in the US, the first meeting we attended, and the first woman I saw, became my wife." Denver returned to Wales only long enough to prepare for his permanent move to the USA. He sailed the second time on the Queen Mary in June of 1956 and married the wonderful Wisconsin-born farm girl turned nurse, Dorothy Hanson, the next month on July 18th. Denver's tag line from this story was this: "God always gives the best to those who leave the choice to Him."

They began their life together in Minneapolis, Minnesota, where Denver was assisting a church, and doing custodial work at a hotel, and Dorothy was employed as a nurse. Not too long after welcoming their son Bill into the world, they responded to a one-year Ministry assignment to help a church in Ontario, Canada. After that year was up, they moved back to the USA, to Dorothy's hometown of Grantsburg, Wisconsin, which would be their home for the following eleven years. Between 1960-1971, four daughters; Mary, Pat, Becky, and Jodi, joined the family and a church, The Wood River Gospel Tabernacle, was planted. "Pioneering work," as Denver called it had no shortage of challenges, yet these were years of great joy and fruitfulness. Living in this quaint and close-knit farming community, being near Dorothy's supportive family, and seeing God bless and grow a fledgling church, created an idyllic setting for the growing Jones family.

In 1971, Denver and his family pulled up stakes and moved to Stewartville, Minnesota to help plant a church and open a bible-training center. Saying goodbye to the people and places they loved was painful. However, the "letting go" of all they held dear of their Grantsburg days paled in comparison to all they were required to release over the next three years in Stewartville. Within the first year, the ministry was languishing, but the most devastating and life-altering event of this confusing season was when Dorothy fought and then lost her battle with breast cancer. Denver, now a grieving widower was left with a failed church plant and five children to raise, ages 1, 7, 10, 12, and 14. These years were Denver's "Dark Night of the Soul." To the family they seemed like one, very long, dark night.

It was in the midst of this emotional and spiritual fog, a lifeline came. Denver received a call from a friend and former missionary, Don Ohman. Don, along with his wife, Dianne, and their 4 children had run an orphanage for Arab boys for 7 years in Ramallah, Jordan (now part of Israel on the West Bank). Don's poor health had forced their return to the USA where they now pastored a church in St Francis, Minnesota. Simply moved by God, Pastor Don reach out to Denver offering friendship, an invitation for Denver to come assist him in his church, and a place for his family to live. Denver and his 4 girls (Bill had joined the Navy by this time) made the move from the big house in Stewartville to a cozy triplex in St Frances, Minnesota. Little did either family know at the time how significant their relationships would become.

Pastor Don truly needed help as his long-term heart condition continued deteriorating. As Don's heart grew weaker, the bond between Denver and

Don grew stronger. Denver considered him his closest friend and was alone with him at the church when he suffered a massive heart attack and died. The two families connected in grief and healed in hope allowing Denver and Dianne to fall in love and marry a year later. With 9 kids between them, Dianne's experience running an orphanage was about to pay off.

A new church plant came on the heels of the wedding. The three oldest kids were already out of the house, leaving 5 teenagers and one 7 year old remaining to live out this wild "Gospel Brady Bunch" adventure. After five blending, blundering, blessed years in Zimmerman, Minnesota, all five teenagers had graduated from High School. By God's grace, the family survived.

In 1982, the next ministry assignment came to pastor a small group of people in Southeast Minnesota who were in the beginning stages of forming a local church. Denver, Dianne, and Jodi moved to Winona, a place they would call home for the next 17 years. Wedding bells rang incessantly over a five-year span, as all 8 adult children were married. Five of these weddings were within 15 months. Dianne deserves a medal of valor for this feat.

Denver spent the remaining years of his life assisting churches, playing with grandkids, and investing in the lives of people. He framed the end of his life with solid hope, always speaking of his own death as "graduation day".

Denver arrived in the U.S with $60.00 in his pocket, and likely had less than that when he died 50 years later at age 85. He realized early on that divine inheritance really has nothing to do with money. It is much more valuable than that. Denver's children and grandchildren grew up hearing that *they* were the "great inheritance" God had promised him. Denver's inheritance: his wife Dianne, 9 children and their spouses, along with 31 grandchildren and many friends, gathered for his "graduation ceremony," and marveled at the faithfulness of God.

Denver Jones Rags and Bones? That depends on the standard of measurement you use. From God's vantage point, Denver entered heaven a very wealthy man. If he were here today, he would tell you that he wasn't a perfect father. However, he would want to make sure you knew that there is a perfect God who loves you with the love of a father, and wants to call you his own.

Our prayer is that these pages will facilitate a clearer, Spirit-born revelation of your very present and loving Heavenly Father.

"I pray that out of his glorious riches he may strengthen you with power through his Spirit in your inner being, so that Christ may dwell in your hearts through faith. And I pray that you, being rooted and established in love, may have power, together with all the Lord's holy people, to grasp how wide and long and high and deep is the love of Christ, and to know this love that surpasses knowledge—that you may be filled to the measure of all the fullness of God. Now to him who is able to do immeasurably more than all we ask or imagine, according to his power that is at work within us, to him be glory in the church and in Christ Jesus throughout all generations, for ever and ever! Amen." –Ephesians 3:15-21

Introduction

— 1 —

"Our Father"

The sight of 30 orphan children sitting on the ground in rapt attention as Becky told one of her "Father Stories" will never leave my mind. Becky and I had taken a ministry trip to assist the Esparza family who are good friends and faithful Pastors in Aguascalientes, Mexico. While there, we were privileged to visit the orphanage they had started many years prior. To add to our delight, our daughter Erin, who lived in Mexico at the time, was with us. Her love for children and near fluency in Spanish made it possible for us to connect and communicate effectively with these precious orphans.

As the sun was setting, we invited the children to gather and be seated. There in the cool twilight of the Mexican countryside and with Erin translating, Becky began sharing a story which is one you will read later in this book. While taking a few steps back to snap a picture and capture this moment, the Spirit of God gripped me deeply. Through tearing eyes I saw these innocent children, each one no doubt coming from a shattered home experience lighting up with a flicker of hope. God was opening their hearts to imagine something previously thought too wonderful. Could God possibly be a good and loving Father... to them? Perhaps this was for some, the beginning of their own journey to the Father's heart.

Jesus Reveals the Father

When Jesus lived on this earth, it seemed His favorite way of addressing God was "Father." We find Him using this intimate title over 165 times in the Gospels. In this, Jesus reveals the Father to us. There is something deeply significant about approaching God with the welcoming descriptor, "Father," on our lips. It sets our relationship in its proper perspective, acknowledging that God, while vastly infinite, is also personally intimate. It allows us to come before him with unfettered hearts, free of all guilt, shame, and fear. It keeps the door of relationship open wide and bids us to freely enter.

Jesus came to restore lost humanity back into sonship with His Father. This deep, spiritual connection transcends even our natural birth and lineage. John writes, *"Yet to all who did receive him, to those who believed in his name, he gave the right to become children of God— children born not of natural descent, nor of human decision or a husband's will, but born of God"* (John 1:12-13). It could be said that the primary focus of Jesus' ministry was to restore the Father-bond we lost in the Garden of Eden. Jesus, as the unique Son of God, was bringing us into a new covenant with the Father - not the old covenant of Law, but one of redemption, grace and sonship!

The disciples witnessed Jesus' intimacy with His Father in prayer and asked that He teach them how to pray. He began His great model prayer with the words, *"Our Father..."* He infers that the first step in our approach to God is a solid awareness that *He is* our spiritual Father. In fact, we cannot have a vibrant, satisfying prayer life unless this reality is settled deep in our hearts. Understanding the following themes of the Lord's Prayer is predicated on how well we understand this first phrase: *"Our Father...."*

Notice that Jesus expresses the entire Lord's Prayer in the *plural*: not *"My"* but "Our" - not *"Me"* but *"Us."* This indicates that we are not in this alone. We are part of the much larger redeemed family of God. Eugene Peterson writes, "With the 'our', Jesus puts Himself in our company. With the 'our', we place ourselves in the company of Jesus and of all who pray." The Creator is not just *my* God or *my* church's God, but the Father of *all* saints in ages past and present. God intended the dynamic of our prayer life to be as His relationship is with us: vast *and* personal.

Some theologians render the first line of the Lord's Prayer like this: *"Our Father, in the very air I breathe, I stop and become aware of You."* (Pause and read that again.) Yes, He is that close to us. In fact, we don't have to "come to God in prayer" because He is already there – as close as the air we breathe! In prayer, we may imagine Him far off in a mystical place beyond our current reality. Yet, the original Greek word we translate "heaven" (*ouranos*) is plural, meaning *"heavens."* The Bible speaks of three heavens: the first heaven, our breathable atmosphere; the air in which the birds fly. The second heaven is the planetary space; celestial home of the stars. The third heaven, the unique abode of God. In prayer, we are addressing our Father who inhabits all of these heavens and is as close to us as our immediate atmosphere! Pastor and author, John Ortberg, beautifully renders this phrase, *"Our Father, who is closer than the air we breathe."* Getting ahold of this will change your prayer life, and how you relate to your Father.

The Gift of "Abba Father"

The Apostle Paul unveils a very significant understanding of our relationship with Father God as he writes to the church in Rome: *"The Spirit you received does not make you slaves, so that you live in fear again; rather, the Spirit you received brought about your adoption to sonship. And by him we cry, 'Abba, Father.' The Spirit himself testifies with our spirit that we are God's children"* (Romans 8:15-16). When we receive Christ as our Savior, we are spiritually adopted into God's family. Our standing in Jesus delivers us from a fear-based life. It removes our sin and shame. The Spirit of God allows us to call out to God as beloved sons and daughters, *"Abba Father!"*

> *"What is a Christian?"* The question can be answered in many ways, but the richest answer I know is that a Christian is one who has God as Father...Our understanding of Christianity cannot be better than our grasp of adoption...The truth of our adoption gives us the deepest insights that the New Testament affords into the greatness of God's love." —J.I. Packer

While Paul was writing in the Greek language, he breaks with it here and inserts the Aramaic word for father: "Abba." Aramaic was the spoken language of Jesus and the common language of Judea in the first century. Some scholars have likened "Abba" to our use of "Daddy" or "Papa," indicating a tender and childlike relationship. Yet, it should be noted that Abba was a term used by both young and adult children for their father. Slaves and household servants were never permitted to use such a familiar, generative term for the master of the house. The biblical use of this word is powerful because it associates us, not as slaves, but as children of the house and heirs of our Father! This is what sets us apart from being merely God's domestic servants. He has given us the privileged status of sonship by which we can freely call Him "Abba!"

Paul immediately follows the Aramaic "Abba" with the Greek word, "Pater" which refers to a begetter, originator, and progenitor. These two terms placed together (here and in Galatians 4:5-7) provide a two-handed grip on our Father God of both intimacy and strength. Interestingly, it was this same double-term title used by Jesus in his prayer of agony in the Garden of Gethsemane: *"Abba, Father," he said, "everything is possible for you. Take this cup from me. Yet not what I will, but what you will"* (Mark 14:36). Jesus had this kind of vital connection to his Father. It was that strength and intimacy that carried him through the pain of the garden and ultimately to the cross. The privilege of knowing God as our Abba Father has been given to us from Christ through the Holy Spirit. Just as Jesus freely addressed God as his Father, we too, can step into the intimacy and strength of this glorious relationship.

If you are a parent, you know that your ears are especially tuned to detect the voice of your own children. Even if you are in a crowded mall or a busy airport surrounded by the low roar of many voices, all it takes to get your immediate attention is for one of your children to let out a "Daddy" or "Mommy." Those who study the brain say that this remarkable ability is a function of our Reticular Activating System (RAS). It helps us decipher between relevant and irrelevant sounds coming into our ears. Our RAS is trained by what we focus on – what is important to us. Now begin to think of God having His RAS attuned to *your* voice. The moment you call out to Him, "Father," you have His undivided attention!

God's Heart Through the Ages

We may wrongly assume that God's Father heart is strictly a New Testament reality. However, closer study shows us otherwise. God's Father heart is foreshadowed throughout the Old Covenant.

Consider our origin in the Garden of Eden. Here we find both man and woman being made in the image and likeness of God (Genesis 1:27-28).

Adam and Eve were given the divine charge to *"Be fruitful and increase in number; fill the earth and subdue it."* Yet, within this context was a nurturing and intimate fatherly relationship with the first couple. Their Creator counseled them, guided them, provided for them, was present with them, disciplined them, and even covered their shame after they had sinned. God reveals Himself from the genesis of our human existence as a good Father.

King David reveals God as a Father to those without their earthly father when he affirms, *"A father to the fatherless, a defender of widows, is God in his holy dwelling. God sets the lonely in families, he leads out the prisoners with singing; but the rebellious live in a sun-scorched land."* Psalm 68:5-6. As the history of the Jewish nation unfolds, Isaiah describes God as a Father to the entire nation. Isaiah 64:8 states, *"Yet you, LORD, are our Father. We are the clay, you are the potter; we are all the work of your hand."* Later, we see the prophet Jeremiah weeping because of the rebellion of the nation of Judah. He was prophesying that God's people would be taken away in exile to Babylon. Through his tears, we get a glimpse into God's father heart for His people: *"I myself said, '"How gladly would I treat you like my children and give you a pleasant land, the most beautiful inheritance of any nation.' I thought you would call me 'Father' and not turn away from following me"* Jeremiah 3:19. This pain-filled groan of God's heart still rings out to all humanity. Hear God's heart toward defeated and broken souls as he calls out, *"I thought you would call me 'Father!"* His heart still reaches out to wayward humanity with the desire to draw us back to Himself. Indeed, life begins for us when we truly call him "Father!"

The Father's All-Encompassing Attributes

Modern liberal theology has blurred the lines of the uniquely male image of God, and we do not want to add to that confusion. He is not a human, confined as we are to our God-given gender, but He is Spirit (John 4:24). He is immortal (I Timothy 6:16). Clearly, both man *and* woman were made in God's likeness (Genesis 1:27). Our natural mothers, as well as fathers, convey and display the many attributes of our Creator (Isaiah 49:14-16). Yet, both Old Testament and New portray God in this male role. The designation of "Father" is not simply a term imposed by the patriarchal culture of biblical times, but it is the proper name for God given in Scripture. It is the best our languages have to portray God as a loving and kind Progenitor. It is how Jesus addressed the first person of the trinity and taught us to do the same. Thus our approach in this book will focus on the distinct role and title of God as our Father while understanding that the natural female attributes of compassion, nurture and tenderness also convey the character of our sovereign God.

Journey Without End

A journey "to" someplace usually suggests there is a point at which we arrive and the journey ends. This is not the case in our walk with God. His infinite glory is beyond our ability to fully grasp. May we never outgrow our childlike wonder of Christ! Whether new in your faith or a veteran believer; whether you have had a great experience with your earthly father or a miserable one, this journey is for you. Open your heart to a fresh impartation from Father God. Ask the Holy Sprit to guide you on this path of discovery. Like the Mexican orphan children gathered around Becky that night, we pray that your heart will come alive to a new understanding of just how good your Father is, and you might dare to breath this prayer on the following page:

Journey to the Father

"God, would you be a good and loving Father to me?"

1: *"Our Father"*

2

Father's Identity

> "God's love did not begin at the cross. It began in eternity before the world was established, before the time clock of civilization began to move." —Billy Graham

Identity, simply put, is who you are. It is the way you think about yourself. Divine identity on the other hand can be defined as who *God* says you are; the way *He* thinks about you. There is a big difference between the two. How we live depends on who (or what) we let define us. Identity apart from God is subjective. Without Him in the equation, our self-perception tends to constantly be in flux, depending on our moods, life experiences and interactions with others. When we come to faith in Christ, we are made holy, but many times, we are still far from being whole. The process of becoming whole has a lot to do with understanding our new identity. Our old identities have become so "us;" we fail to see they are false and based on lies. For example: a person who experienced childhood abandonment or rejection may grow up believing they are unimportant and unlovable. Our freedom as believers comes as we identify and replace those lies with what is true according to God's Word. Jesus said, *"Then you will know the truth, and the truth will set you free."* John 8:32

> *"Though our feelings come and go, God's love for us does not."*
> —C.S. Lewis

Our search for identity apart from Christ is unending. We make guesswork out of what we were designed to confidently know: We were *created* by God, to be *loved* by God, for the *purpose* of God.

*"For you created my inmost being; you knit me together in my mother's womb. I praise you because I am fearfully and wonderfully made; your works are wonderful, I **know** that full well"* (Psalm 139:13-14). This *knowing* comes by revelation of the Holy Spirit and goes beyond mere mental assent. We see this in Paul's prayer for the Ephesians. *"And I pray that you, being rooted and established in love, may have power [by the Spirit]...to grasp how wide and long and high and deep is the love of Christ, and to know this love that surpasses knowledge"* (Ephesians 3:17b-19). This unusual kind of "knowledge" is better understood through the original Greek word used: **"ginóskó,"** which indicates a knowledge based on personal experience. Because the love of God is beyond natural comprehension, it is grasped in its fullness only as it is *experienced*. The simple children's song, "Jesus Loves Me" becomes a profound anthem when we go from Jesus loves me this I *hope* to Jesus loves me this I *know*!

God is the only one who can meet our deepest needs. We are designed by God to be fulfilled by Him. John Piper puts the implications of this truth succinctly, "What we don't freely receive from God, we demand from others." Don't miss this; to the degree our identity is grounded on who God says we are is the degree we are able to let others off the hook to satisfy us!

As Christ followers, we must confidently know that love is what motivated God's redemptive plan. John 3:16 says, *"For God **so loved** the world that he gave his one and only Son, that whoever believes in him shall not perish but have eternal life."* God's love for all of humanity was at the heart of Jesus'

2: Father's Identity – "My Daddy Calls Me Love"

life, ministry and mission. Understanding and personally receiving the divine, unconditional love of our Father is our *first* step and accompanies *every* step as we grow in our faith. Thus, it is here that we will start our journey to the Father's heart.

As you read the following recollection of Becky's childhood experience, consider how great is the Father's love for *you*.

My Daddy Calls Me Love

I had gotten the privilege of tagging along with Mom on her Saturday grocery-shopping trip to the Alpha Store, four miles down the road from our Wisconsin farm. The little village of Alpha was one of those places where the saying, "if you blink you'll miss it," is fitting. The only thing in Alpha besides Alpha store was an elementary school, a church, a cheese factory, and a feed mill; all which were in close enough proximity to be in full view from the store's front door. We lived in this quaint and peaceful farming community, seemingly preserved from the scene of an old movie set, at a time when children could wander at will, causing no alarm to their parents. The only cause for parental alarm, in fact, was that their children might misbehave. The deterrent in the mind of us children, however, was the knowledge that any of our mischief would be quickly discovered and dealt with by whomever's parent happened to be watching. It seemed parents were omnipresent and in cahoots with child rearing in those days making it difficult for us children to get away with much of anything!

Alpha store was frequented regularly by the town's folk as much for social engagement as for checking off a shopping list. Conversations flowed easily as friends and acquaintances exchanged bits of news and family happenings with one another. We children appreciated the extra time these neighborly visits gave us to explore. Besides groceries, this "general store," carried: bib overalls, gardening tools, fly swatters, the gamut of basic necessities. While our parents gathered what it was they needed, we kids could usually be found in one of two places: looking, with fascination, in the section where delightful little trinkets and gifts were displayed or at my favorite post: the penny candy counter. I could stand there indefinitely, peering longingly at all the neatly arranged rows of brightly colored candy. It was a beautiful sight to behold, *and* it was all within reach. So close but yet so far away!

This particular day, as I was dreamily gazing at the candy and deeply contemplating which one to choose if given the opportunity, Gordon, the friendly owner of the establishment, came over to where I was standing. "Excuse me, young lady," he said in the least startling way possible, "but can I ask your name?" The response to that question spilled out naturally and matter-of-factly. "My name is Becky," I answered, "but my daddy calls me love." Amused and evidently charmed by this unexpected response, he returned to his work smiling broadly and chuckling to himself.

Dad, having been born and raised in Wales, Great Britain, still carried his rich Welsh accent along with various customs, terms and expressions from the old country. It wasn't until my first visit to Wales as a freshman in high school I realized that Dad's "oddities" were mostly just Welsh traditions. For example, in Wales, everyone calls everyone "love," even perfect strangers. It was a cultural thing that I had taken personally for the first 14 years of my life.

2: Father's Identity – *"My Daddy Calls Me Love"*

Consider the implications of such a bold and instinctive response to our Heavenly Father who *always* intends for us to take His love personally. Dare we believe it possible? If so, it would change the way we live. Honestly, it's sometimes easier for me to accept, believe, and receive the love of God in a cultural, "For God so loved the world" kind of way than a personal, "For God so loved Becky" kind of way; how about you? *(Insert your name in the following statement.)*

"*My name is* _____
but my Daddy calls me love."

Can you receive it? It's the truth, and it's sweeter than penny candy!

Little Becky Jones believed that what her dad *called* her was actually *true of* her. "Love," instead of merely being a popular British expression became a very personal identity. Our Heavenly Father desires the same for us: *"How great is the love the Father has lavished on us, that we should be called children of God! And that is what we are"* (I John 3:1). In Christ, we are lavishly loved and have standing favor with God. This love cannot be earned. It is not based on our own merit, goodness, or performance. In fact, any effective service for God flows from a revelation of His boundless love for us. May we believe it and receive it from Him fully and freely.

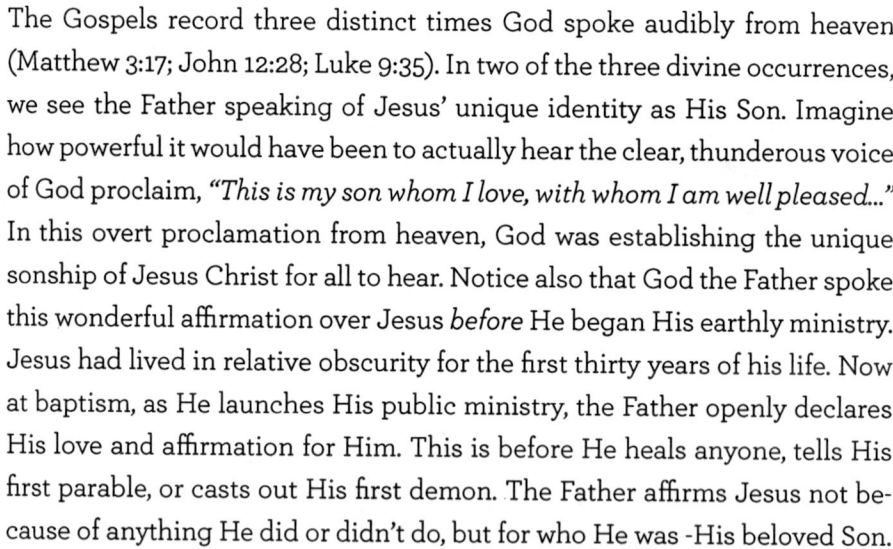

"Long before any human being saw us, we are seen by God's loving eyes. Long before anyone heard us cry or laugh, we are heard by our God who is all ears for us. Long before any person spoke to us in this world, we are spoken to by the voice of eternal love." – Henri Nouwen

The Gospels record three distinct times God spoke audibly from heaven (Matthew 3:17; John 12:28; Luke 9:35). In two of the three divine occurrences, we see the Father speaking of Jesus' unique identity as His Son. Imagine how powerful it would have been to actually hear the clear, thunderous voice of God proclaim, *"This is my son whom I love, with whom I am well pleased..."* In this overt proclamation from heaven, God was establishing the unique sonship of Jesus Christ for all to hear. Notice also that God the Father spoke this wonderful affirmation over Jesus *before* He began His earthly ministry. Jesus had lived in relative obscurity for the first thirty years of his life. Now at baptism, as He launches His public ministry, the Father openly declares His love and affirmation for Him. This is before He heals anyone, tells His first parable, or casts out His first demon. The Father affirms Jesus not because of anything He did or didn't do, but for who He was -His beloved Son.

Christian friend, as those who have repented of sin and asked for the forgiveness of God through the sacrificial death of Jesus, we also have a standing of lavish favor before God. When we first open our eyes in the morning, before we do anything good or bad, our Father in heaven delights over us.

His love is beyond comprehension and the depth of His kindness cannot be plumbed. This is our spiritual birthright, and we must not let our own sense of unworthiness or Satan's lies steal it from us.

Just forty days after Jesus' baptism, the devil came to tempt Him in the wilderness. Satan moved to undermine the very revelation of Jesus' divine identity. Take note of what the tempter said to Jesus: *"if you are the son of God..."* Just as Satan came against what God spoke about Jesus, he also seeks to cast doubt on our identity in Christ. We must resist him by standing on God's Word in the face of this onslaught as Jesus did. We too must have on our lips, *"It is written"* when we battle for our standing as sons and daughters of God.

Jesus chose twelve disciples to be with Him, learn from Him, and carry His message to the ends of the earth. One of those disciples was a young man named John. Six times in the Gospel bearing his name, John refers to himself as *"the disciple whom Jesus loved."* Was this arrogance, insecurity or pride on John's part? Or was it the fact that he understood and entered into this divine love so fully and personally that he could humbly identify himself this way? To say that you are the "disciple whom Jesus loved" does not imply that Jesus did not love the other disciples; rather, it shows that John was able to intimately receive and appropriate this love he knew to be vast as an ocean. In this man, we see a unique ability to receive from Jesus. Three times in the Gospels we read of Jesus leaving the other disciples behind and only inviting Peter, James and John along. It was John who leaned against Jesus at the last supper. At the foot of the cross, John and Mary, Jesus' mother, stood in grief. There, Jesus placed the care of His mother into the hands of John when He said, *"Woman, here is your son,"* and to the disciple, *"Here is your mother." From that time on, this disciple took her into his home"* (John 19:26-27). It was John who is attributed with writing the Gospel bearing his name, First, Second, and Third John, as well as the book of Revelation, five canonized books in all. Like John, we can also have a great kingdom impact if we believe that we are a "disciple who Jesus loves."

There is something very powerful about personally and unapologetically receiving the love of God. In my mother's home hangs a plaque that says: "God loves you, but I'm His favorite." Don't you love that? We should be able to say that as well. This revelation of divine love took the Apostle John into his ninety-third year – the longest living disciple of Jesus. It brought him through severe persecutions, imprisonment, exile, and trials as a victor. At the end of his life, he was not a bitter old man. Church history tells the story of "blessed John the evangelist" in extreme old age at Ephesus. He was carried into the congregation in the arms of his disciples unable to say anything except, "Little children, love one another."

The Gospel of Christ is founded on the great love of God for us. Can we, like little Becky, so appropriate our Father's love that it transforms our very self-perception? Your Father calls *you* 'Love.'

Get into the Story:

1. Do you base your identity more on how your Heavenly Father sees you or how you feel about yourself? What are some of your self-perceptions that need to be adjusted by the truth of God's Word?

2: Father's Identity – *"My Daddy Calls Me Love"*

2. Satan's words still ring in our own minds, *"If you are a child of God…"* In what ways has he sought to undermine your true identity in Christ?

3. Write out and commit to memory a key Scripture that will help you stand confidently in your identity as a lavishly loved child of God.

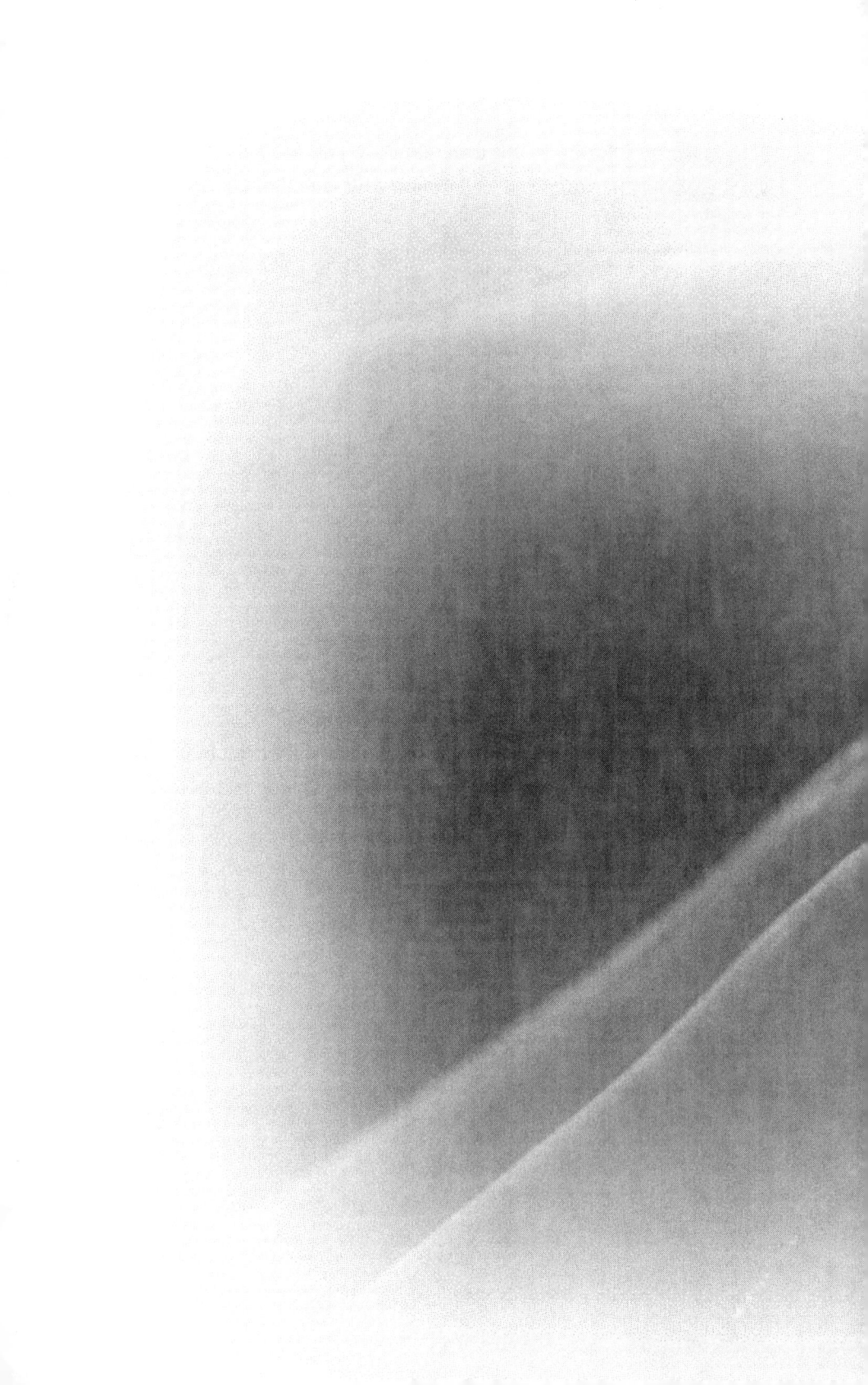

~ 3 ~

Father's Acceptance

> "Tell fearful souls,
> "Courage! Take heart!
> God is here, right here,
> on his way to put things right
> And redress all wrongs.
> He's on his way! He'll save you!"
>
> —Isaiah 35:4 (The Message)

Perhaps one of the most sinister weapons against the human soul is shame. Second only to fear, shame has been our arch nemesis from the beginning of time. We met shame in the Garden of Eden when our first parents were deceived and sinned against God. They made fig leaf clothes to cover their nakedness and hid from God. Before sin, this was their reality: *"Adam and his wife were both naked, and they **felt no shame**"* (Genesis 2:25).

For many of us, shame exists as a nagging feeling just under the surface of our conscious soul. It is the disease within a closed heart that robs our spiritual confidence, deflates our hope, and steals our joy. It has become like an unwelcome houseguest, taking up residence where it has not been invited and has no right to be. Shame hinders our ability to relate to others in a healthy way - driving us to either shut down with feelings of inadequacy or power up to compensate for insecurity. Most sadly, shame keeps us from enjoying God as our Father and approaching Him freely. Adam and Eve taught us well with their very natural response to shame: cover, hide, blame.

Brene' Brown in her book, *Daring Greatly*, gives us a potent definition of shame: "I believe that there is a profound difference between shame and guilt. I believe that guilt is adaptive and helpful – it's holding something we've done or failed to do up against our values and feeling psychological discomfort. I define shame as the intensely painful feeling or experience of believing that we are flawed and therefore unworthy of love and belonging – something we've experienced, done, or failed to do makes us unworthy of connection." Did you catch the hidden nugget in her definition of shame? It makes us feel that we are *"unworthy of connection."* This is why it is so destructive for a Christian to live with the controlling influence of shame in their soul. Christ came to restore the connection to God we lost in the Garden of Eden.

While shame is devastating, it is an appropriate response of a broken soul. Shame realizes its sense of unworthiness before a perfect and holy God. However, there is more to the story. In the Garden of Eden, God foreshadowed how He would remove our shame and atone for our sin by being the first to shed blood to make garments of skin for Adam and Eve (Genesis 3:1). It is only by the shedding of blood that sin is covered (Hebrews 9:24). The cornerstone of the Gospel is found in 2 Corinthians 5:21, *"God made him who had no sin to be sin for us, so that in him we might become the righteousness of God."*

It is truly powerful when we live shameless before God. Shame and its cousin, condemnation, have been dealt with at the cross of Christ. Romans 8:1 declares, *"Therefore, there is now no condemnation for those who are in Christ Jesus."* Only in Jesus are we truly able to live without shame.

One of Satan's titles is *"the accuser of our brothers and sisters"* (Revelation 12:10). God's answer to our accuser is what the Bible calls 'justification,' meaning that we are declared legally righteous before God. The Apostle Paul sets forth the power of the Gospel in Romans 5:1-2 when he says, *"Therefore, since we have been justified through faith, we have peace with God through our Lord Jesus Christ, through whom we have gained access by faith into this grace in which we now stand."* Notice that this justification has given us "access" into God's grace. What Adam and Eve lost as they were expelled from the garden has been restored through Christ. God has given us access to come before him with no shame. Ephesians 3:12 declares, *" In him [Christ] and through faith in him we may approach God with freedom and confidence."*

Yet, even in light of the Gospel's clear claims, many of us find it hard to come out from under a cloud of shame. We try to remove it with spiritual commitment, service or devotion, but these are only covers for a deeper root lying within. Martin Luther addresses this when he says, "The sin underneath all our sins is to trust the lie of the serpent that we cannot trust the love and grace of Christ and must take matters into our own hands." We must learn who and what defines us. It is not our past achievements or failures, our hurts, wounds, relationships, things done or things we've done to others. Our Father defines us based on the merits of Christ.

Now, lets discover the powerful truth of the Father's unconditional acceptance with the following story of four-year-old Becky Jones.

Horsy Rides in the Holy of Holies

Hearing the sounds of Dad praying are one of my earliest memories. I use "sounds" intentionally because more often than not, his prayers were expressed with groans as much as with words. We lived in the old Wisconsin farmhouse where my mom grew up. I don't know which groaned louder, my Dad's prayers or the floorboards in the upstairs hallway. My parent's bedroom was situated in the middle of the hallway between the room I shared with my two older sisters, Mary and Pat, and our older brother, Bill. The groaning of the floorboards made it impossible to sneak passed Mom and Dad's room. Believe me, we tried!

One day, I found my four-year-old self alone in the hallway outside the door of my parent's bedroom, listening to Dad pray. I knew by the travailing tones I heard on the other side of the door that something very important and personal was going on. Certainly, my presence would be an intrusion. But this particular time, my curiosity got the best of me. I found myself opening the door, just a crack, to have a peek into the "holy of holies."

There was Dad, by his bed, on his knees, head buried in his folded hands. The farmhouse was as drafty as it was creaky, so my Dad would often have a blanket draped over his shoulders. In my childish imagination, it appeared as a priestly garment of some sort. Between the groaning hallway floor and the squeaky bedroom door, I was discovered immediately. I realized at that point I didn't have a plan beyond the peek, so I just stood there, frozen, with a strained smile on my face, looking as innocent as possible. Was I in trouble? Would he send me away? Could I "enter the holy of holies and live"?

Dad lifted his bowed head. Had he expected to see an angel? All I know is that when his eyes fell on me, they were smiling. He motioned for me to come to over to him. He was already on his knees so it took little effort for him to scoot me up on his back. From there he proceeded to give me a horsy ride around the room. I was delighted! It didn't

I believe my Dad wasn't the only Father smiling that day!

take too many laps before I was satisfied and on my way out the door to find someone else to interrupt.

Looking back on this experience, I realize that the idea of my presence being an intrusion was in my mind alone. His consistent welcoming response to my invasion of his personal space reinforced what is true of our Heavenly Father. He loves being with us. He invites us to draw near, and stay near: confident of His love and free of guilt and shame.

I didn't realize it at the time, but Dad's response also taught me a lasting spiritual lesson regarding true spirituality. He didn't have to shift gears from travailing prayer to playing with me, as if moving from something more spiritual to less spiritual. He didn't feel the need to make this a "religious experience" by expounding doctrine or teaching me the virtues of prayer. He knew that I simply desired to be with him. Holiness in those fleeting moments was a horsey ride.

Journey to the Father

God, our Father, delights to receive us into His presence without shame. In fact, the somberness we sometimes anticipate as we approach God may turn into a veritable horsey ride around the Holy of Holies! When we pray, we are directed in Scripture to do so with full confidence. Hebrews 4:16 says, *"Let us then approach God's throne of grace with confidence, so that we may receive mercy and find grace to help us in our time of need."* This confidence is not arrogance or an attitude of entitlement, rather, it is a supreme reliance on God's Fatherly acceptance of us in Christ.

Denver surprised Becky by signaling her over to him with a smile. Why? Because he delighted in her. He enjoyed her presence and she did his. We may wrongly think that our relationship with God is all one sided. We give Him all the bad stuff; He gives us all the good stuff. But, could it be that He actually delights in our relationship with him? Zephaniah 3:17 speaks of the restoration of God's people with these words: *"The LORD your God is with you, the Mighty Warrior who saves. He will take great delight in you; in his love he will no longer rebuke you, but will rejoice over you with singing."*

It says your Father "will take great delight in you." The original Hebrew root word here carries the thought of dancing over you, leaping for joy and spinning under the influence of a violent emotion! Further, this verse describes God as singing over us with great joy. Our redemption doesn't bring us into God's begrudging approval but into his jubilant acceptance.

Why is it so important to know our Father's unconditional and joyful acceptance? Because we can only reflect to others the image we personally hold of our Heavenly Father. The late Bible teacher Jack Frost wrote, "You will treat yourself and others according to the way you think God feels about you." If our perception of God is tainted, it will tarnish the way we live our lives and relate to others. However, if we understand that God's heart toward us is delightfully welcoming, we will extend this welcoming grace to others.

Next time you are tempted to tiptoe past your Father's chambers, stop to consider His great love for you. Crack the door open, peek in, see His smile, and approach Him with confidence, and get ready for the best "horsey ride" you ever had!

> "We should be astonished at the goodness of God, stunned that He should bother to call us by name, our mouths wide open at His love, bewildered that at this very moment we are standing on holy ground."
> —Brennan Manning

Get into the Story:

1. Shame makes us feel that we are "unworthy of connection." Describe a time when shame has driven you from relationship with God or others.

2. Hebrews 4:16 tells us that we can approach God with confidence because of Christ. How confident are you in your personal prayer and worship to your Father?

3. Is it difficult for you to picture your Heavenly Father rejoicing over you with singing and dancing as described in Zephaniah 3:17? Why or why not?

3: Father's Acceptance – *"Horsey Rides in the Holy of Holies"*

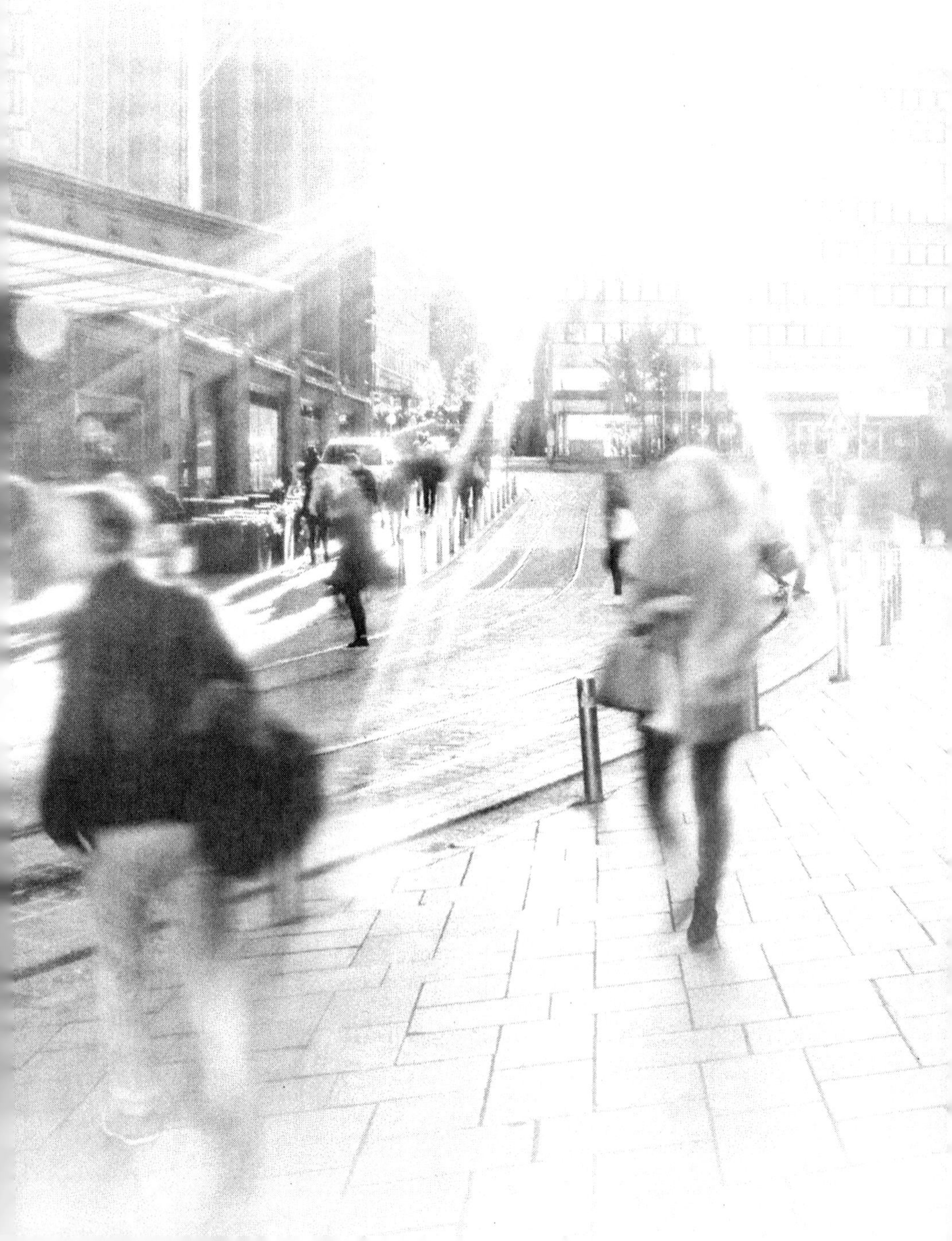

4

Father's Care

> "Lost people matter to God, and so they must matter to us."
> —Keith Wright

The most quoted verse in the Bible gives us the most basic motivation of our Heavenly Father.

"For God so loved the world..." (John 3:16). God's deep love for the people of the world was the driving force behind Him sending Jesus Christ to earth. We can enter into His agenda by being attentive to the people around us. God's plan is to show His love *for* people *through* other people. Whether large or small, our mindfulness in word and deed can express the heart of God for the people He puts in our path.

Journey to the Father

Have you ever been in a hurry while out shopping only to spot someone you know from across the store? Perhaps it is a neighbor or a friend from church. It may be an acquaintance from work or even a family member. In that frenzied moment you have a decision to make: say hello and risk a longer than desired conversation, or dart into the nearest "safety zone," which may happen to be the cat food isle. You may not want to admit you would ever do such a thing, but it is actually a common response among kind but time-crunched people.

Life's pressure-cooker pace pushes us to check off our to-do list rather than checking in with the people around us, to be productive over being present. Technology can give us a sense of being connected as 'friends' all the while taking us away from truly *being* a friend. Our world is so full of busyness and noise that we rarely pause to listen to God, others, or our own thoughts for that matter. Chances are we've likely forgotten altogether what silence sounds like. "Sadly," says James Dobson, "this overcommitted and breathless way of life, which I call 'routine panic,' characterizes the vast majority of people in Western nations." He maintains that it is a main contributing factor in the breakdown of family relationships today. Certainly, we would be wise to consider how our *pace of life* is affecting our *quality of life*.

> "I cannot think of a single advantage I've ever gained from being in a hurry. But a thousand broken and missed things, tens of thousands, lie in the wake of all the rushing.... Through all that haste I thought I was making up time. It turns out I was throwing it away." —Ann Voskamp

Nowhere in the Gospels do we read anything like, *"Having been detained by the Pharisees, Jesus rushed across town because He was in a hurry to heal a man who was blind from birth."* Jesus was often busy, but Scripture never shows him hurried. There was even a time when there were so many people coming to Him that He and the disciples had no time to eat (Mark 6:31). Yes, there are times when we will have to act quickly to be good stewards of our time, but a harried lifestyle is a sickness of the soul. Yet, Jesus,

4: Father's Care – "The Saving Qualities of Tea"

the man, accomplished more in 3 years of earthly ministry than any one of us could accomplish in a lifetime. What was His secret? He was on His Father's schedule, looking to do only what was given Him for that moment (John 5:19). He was not driven by the expectations of others. Jesus was a man who knew how to be fully present in every moment.

Pastor John Ortberg tells of his meeting with a counselor to get help with maintaining spiritual balance in the midst of a very busy ministry schedule. He described the many demands of family life, soccer games, piano lessons, school orientation meetings, etc. Now, with pen in hand, he wanted to get all the wisdom he could so he asked his wise mentor, "So, what must I do to be spiritually healthy?" After a long pause, his counselor said, "You must ruthlessly eliminate hurry from your life" Then more silence for a long time.... "Okay, I've written that one down," John told him, "That's a good one. Now what else is there?" Then another long pause. "There is nothing else," he said. "You must ruthlessly eliminate hurry from your life." Think about the pace of your life right now. Are you presently in a season where this advice is needed?

We can be encouraged by what Jesus modeled *and* invites us to: a life marked by a graceful flow of fruitful ministry. He says in Matthew 11:28-30 *"Come to me, all you who are weary and burdened, and I will give you rest. Take my yoke upon you and learn from me, for I am gentle and humble in heart, and you will find rest for your souls. For my yoke is easy and my burden is light."* It is helpful on occasion to take a serious inventory of our souls. Are we weary and burdened, stressed, and on the verge of burnout? Whose yoke is on our shoulders? Is it a heavy yoke formed by the expectations of others or ourselves or is it the light and well-fitted yoke fashioned for us by Jesus?

When I was young in the ministry and filled with more zeal than wisdom, my idea of fruitfulness was to fill my calendar with one activity, outing, or outreach after another. I was a hard-charging, type A leader high on advancing God's cause on earth. I got frustrated with anyone who got in my way or didn't run at my speed. Discerning my pace of ministry, a wise teacher offered me a gem of wisdom. He said, "When we work, God rests, but when we rest, God works." That little nugget of truth impacted my life and has informed the way I do ministry. My ambitions to accomplish set up a false finish line. Now, by God's grace, I let Him set the finish lines and define the "wins."

The most obvious indication of a rushed life is that we do not authentically exhibit the fruit of the Spirit. How does a harried and beleaguered person truly live a life of love, joy, peace, patience, kindness, goodness, faithfulness, gentleness and self-control (Galatians 5:22-23)? These fruits are evidences of the Spirit living through us. Notice that each tend to be a relationship-oriented virtue. The beauty of a Spirit-controlled life is actually others-centered; people around us get to enjoy our fruit. Perhaps the greatest benefit of a non-rushed life is that it allows us to invest in what really matters: people.

"The Saving Qualities of Tea"

My dad was a pastor and loved "going visiting". We (usually some of us kids were along) would get in the car and stop in at people's homes, unannounced to visit. The concept is quite unusual today, but at that time, it seemed acceptable. The folks we visited weren't necessarily from our church. I remember being in the home of my kindergarten teacher, Mrs. Baker, whose little yellow house was as tidy and cheery as her classroom. Sometimes we visited our school bus driver, Orlin Johnson. He had boys who always seemed to be in need of haircuts. Dad took the opportunity on those "pastoral visits" to practice his barbering skills. Much to the dismay of the boys, the long visits usually resulted in hair too short for their liking.

It's uncanny, as I think about our visits, how many of these people not only invited us into their homes, but most of them had food on hand and offered us something to eat; It was usually something freshly baked *and* homemade. They didn't even know we were coming! Of course the sweet treats were what made "visiting" so much fun as far as us kids were concerned, but after several visits, we were ready to do something different like go home and play.

It was a well-known fact in our small, Scandinavian, coffee-drinking community that dad was a tea-drinking Welshman. They might have held it against him had it not been for the woman he married. My mom was a home-town girl...one of their "own kind," known and loved. Thankfully, they quickly forgave the Welsh part and simply learned to offer her husband tea instead of coffee.

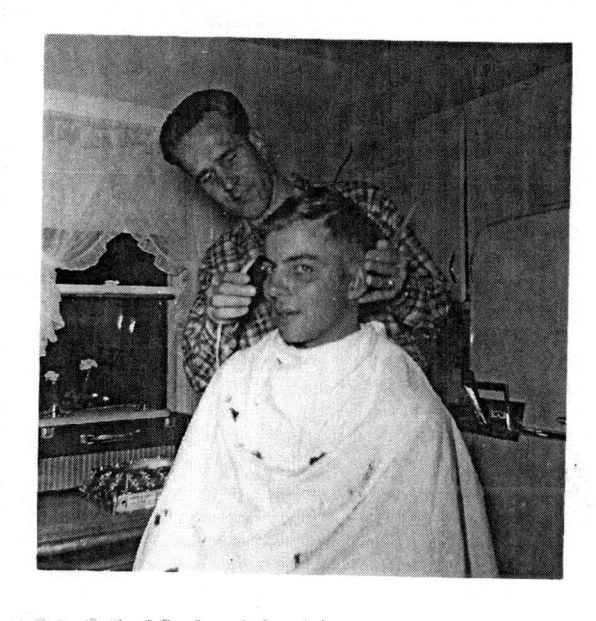

These visits were sometimes deliberate and sometimes spontaneous As far as Dad was concerned, any time was a good time for visiting. Us kids, however, didn't always share the same level of passion. "Dad, do we *have* to stop?" we'd ask. "Just two minutes," he'd say. That never brought any measure of comfort; Welsh minutes must have been longer than American minutes! Whatever the case, we would always follow up his "two minutes" comment with a second plea. "Dad, when they ask if you want tea, *please* say no." It was inevitable; Mrs. Johnson/Jorgensen/Olson/Peterson/Hanson would greet us at her door. "Why, Mr. Jones," they'd say, "how nice to see you. Won't you come in for a cup of tea?" We'd be holding our breath, hoping against hope he would cordially decline, but it was always the same answer, "Thank you, we'd love to." We, his little flock, would follow him through the door and find our places. I don't remember the conversations shared on those visits, but there was always mention or demonstration of the love of Jesus and the offer of prayer.

There is still "fruit that remains" in many of the families we visited all those years ago. Orlin the bus driver and his family are one example. Dad eventually had the privilege of leading them to Christ. The boys may have considered Dad's haircuts too *short*, but the impact of his neighborly kindness went *long*.

I learned something from all those visits: pure and simple, people matter to God.

When it comes to subordinating our schedule to being truly present with the people around us, we must build in times for "divine interruptions." Denver Jones was often heard saying, "I was *born* to be interrupted." I guess at some point he just surrendered and considered it a calling. Normally, an interruption in our daily routine is a threat to our productivity. What would happen if we willingly placed ourselves at God's disposal giving Him the right to change and redirect our plans? Jesus wonderfully modeled this yielding to His Father's agenda. In John 5, we read about one of His "interruptions," which resulted in the healing of a crippled man. This was Jesus' response to the disgruntled Jewish leaders who were upset that He had healed someone on the Sabbath: *"Very truly I tell you, the Son can do nothing by himself; he can do only what he sees his Father doing, because whatever the Father does the Son also does. For the Father loves the Son and shows him all he does"* (John 5:19-20).

Picking up on these divine interruptions requires sensitivity to the Spirit's voice, courage to move into someone's life, and an overarching love and compassion for all people. This love is contrary to our human nature, but it is available to us in Christ. We are reminded of this in Romans 5:5: *"... God's love has been poured out into our hearts through the Holy Spirit, who has been given to us."* What a great *and* desperately needed reminder; We have been given a love beyond our own from which to draw! Divine interruptions are not inconveniences, but invitations from God to be His hands extended. He is behind them and working through us to be light in darkness, sweetness in bitterness, and hope in despair. I John 3:18 challenges our good intentions to take on shoe leather: *"Dear children, let us not love with words or speech but with actions and in truth."*

There is much being written in these days about presence – the ability to be fully engaged, intentionally mindful, compassionate and available to others. Or as the late missionary, Jim Elliot said, "Wherever you are, be *all there."* Just think of what this means to all of us addicted to our smart phones. Rather than looking down at our handheld devices, may we look up into the faces God has placed before us. John Eldredge writes, "The gift of presence is a rare and beautiful gift. To come - unguarded, undistracted - and be fully present, fully engaged with whoever we are with at that moment." Don't miss out on your ministry of "presence" – it is both an act of love and the selfless delivery system of true compassion.

All of this requires a mind subdued by God's gentle Spirit. If our soul is a tornado, then the path we leave behind is strewn with turmoil. Yet, when our inner life has been quieted, our ambitions subordinated, and our opinions humbled, we can begin to be truly helpful to others. The Apostle Paul challenges us to not live for ourselves, doing what we want, but to live by the Spirit when he writes, *"You, my brothers and sisters, were called to be free. But do not use your freedom to indulge the flesh; rather, serve one another humbly in love... So I say, walk by the Spirit, and you will not gratify the desires of the flesh. For the flesh desires what is contrary to the Spirit, and the Spirit what is contrary to the flesh. They are in conflict with each other, so that you are not to do whatever you want"* (Galatians 5:13, 16-17).

So the next time you are nudged by the Holy Spirit to "go visiting," be alert, attentive, and present. Say, "yes" to the invitation to linger over a cup of tea. You may be surprised at its saving qualities.

> *"Let no one ever come to you without leaving better and happier. Be the living expression of God's kindness: kindness in your face, kindness in your eyes, kindness in your smile."* —Mother Teresa

4: Father's Care – *"The Saving Qualities of Tea"*

Get into the Story:

1. How "driven by hurry" is your life? What can you do to build in margin for divine interruptions?

2. How can the phrase, *"When we work, God rests, but when we rest, God works"* help you become a person of greater peace?

3. "When our inner life has been quieted, our ambitions subordinated, and our opinions humbled, we can begin to be truly helpful to others." How true is this of your life?

4: Father's Care – *"The Saving Qualities of Tea"*

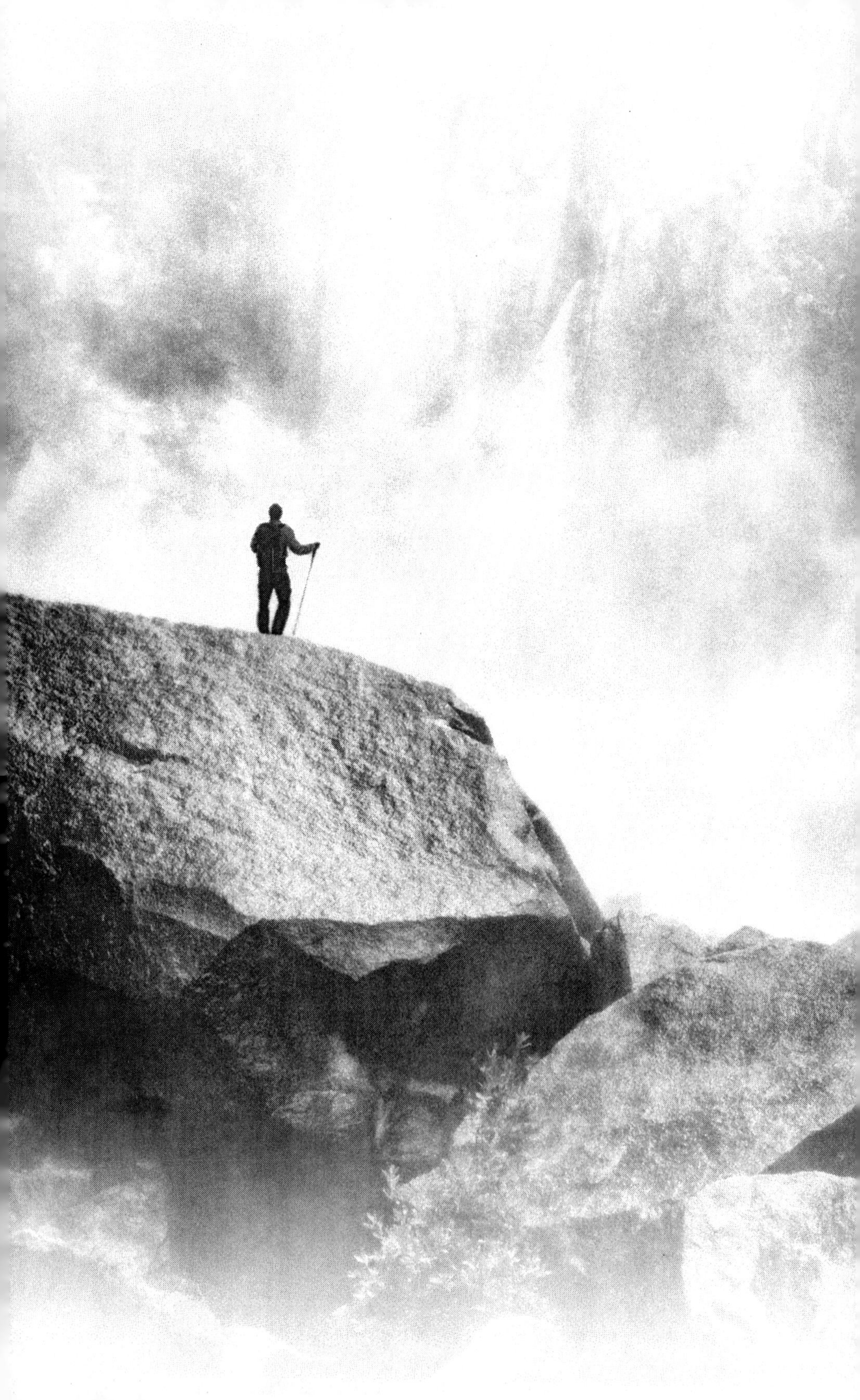

5

Father's Delight

> *"God delights in pouring His favor on obedient risk-takers."* —Bill Hybels

Are you the type of person who runs *into* or *from* the spotlight? Depending on our personality, the thought of being the center of attention either energizes or terrifies us. As comedian Jerry Seinfeld has said, "According to most studies, people's number one fear is public speaking. Number two is death. Death is number two! Does that sound right? This means to the average person, if you go to a funeral, you're better off in the casket than doing the eulogy!" Extroverts love standing before a crowd; introverts avoid it at all costs. One is not better than the other, and there's nothing sweeter than feeling at home in our own skin; but "being on display" becomes complicated when the estimation of ourselves is off-center.

Often lurking at the root of such a dilemma is humanity's age-old stumbling block: pride. For the one who yearns for the spotlight, pride says, "I've got this! I am important because people love paying attention to me." To the one who runs from the spotlight, pride says, "I could never do this! Unimportant as I am, no one would ever want to pay attention to me." The problem with both of these unhealthy mindsets is that it's still all about I and me. Ultimately, pride is at the root of a self-focused life. The only hope of deliverance, in this case, is having a heart attitude of Christ-centered self-forgetfulness.

It is our observation that God's most faithful and effective servants, in biblical history as well as in church history, were initially very reluctant to step into what God had called them to be and do. In other words, they stepped into serving God's purpose only after being severely worked over by the Lord. Consider God's call to Moses at the burning bush in Exodus chapter 3. There we see Moses in a literal argument with God over going back to Egypt to represent God's people to Pharaoh. At the end of the deliberation, Moses sidesteps and essentially says, "Okay, God, I hear your point, but send Aaron, not me!" Thankfully, God eventually persuaded Moses, allowing Aaron to be his assistant, and the rest is biblical history.

Much of modern Christianity focuses on a message of self-actualization, self-expression, and self-fulfillment. These have some value, of course, but what will truly take us into the fullness of God's purpose is self-forgetfulness. Consider this oft-quoted line from Irenaeus, an early church father, who said, "The glory of God is man fully alive." Our "aliveness" is not about our own self-actualization, but rather about God's life being expressed through our redeemed soul. This is how God is fully glorified in us. Whether showy or shy, pride is at work; it is not until we truly "get over ourselves" that we can be fully used by God.

When God needed a mouthpiece for Israel, he asked, *"Whom shall I send? And who will go for us?"* It was Isaiah the prophet who famously answered, *"Here am I. Send me!"* God's prophet was only brought to that place of willingness *after* experiencing a terrifying revelation of God's glory that he was sure would kill him. He saw the grandeur of God so powerfully that it shook the temple where he was standing to its very foundation. Just as he was convinced of his utter uncleanness, the angel flew over to him and touched his lips with a hot coal from the altar to atone for his sin. See Isaiah 6:1-8. Similarly, we are able to answer God's call best only after we have been undone and delivered from our greatest fears.

This is the perspective of David when he penned this great song: Psalm 8:4-6 *"What is mankind that you are mindful of them, human beings that you care for them? You have made them a little lower than the angels and crowned them with glory and honor. You made them rulers over the works of your hands; you put everything under their feet."* Here, David begins by marveling at God's condescension toward our lowly lives and ends with the fact that we are crowned with glory and honor. Holding these two truths in proper tension is vital to finding our place in God's purpose for us on earth.

This was one of the ultimate lessons Becky and her sisters learned while up on the stage of their father's delight. While at times painfully embarrassing, there is a timeless gem to be found on the other side of "awkward."

"Front and Center"

If there was a platform in sight, Dad somehow managed to get us kids standing up on it. If there wasn't, a makeshift one would do. And what did we do while standing in such elevated places you might ask? Most often we would sing, although *what* we did or how *well* we did it didn't seem to matter so much to Dad. He simply delighted in us and took every opportunity to "display his splendor." He called it "lawful pride."

We spent considerable time in nursing homes standing on piano benches. From there we'd smile big and sing our hearts out. The residents loved it, hearing loss notwithstanding, and rewarded us with round pink candies that tasted like Pepto Bismol.

Then, there was the church. We stood behind pulpits and upon platforms and pews far and wide delivering our smiles, songs, and sentiments. I remember an experience where a swell of snickering rose from some of the congregants with whom we were sharing our God-given talents. We wondered what in the world was causing their embarrassing response. We painfully endured the rest of the church service before finding out what had happened. While we were singing, our sister Jodi (then three years old) had seated herself on a railing in front of the pulpit, which had hidden her from our view. There she proceeded to unpack her little purse, lining its contents up in a neat row along the railing. Obviously in her own world... and having a great time, she managed to have everything back in the purse by the end of our song. My sisters and I were ready to crawl *under* the pews as we descended the stage that day, but Dad wasn't bothered. In fact he seemed to rather enjoy it.

Another time we found ourselves playing guitar and singing on the stage of a fancy California hotel. We were there attending a large evangelistic crusade. I can't imagine what Dad said to the crusade organizer to schedule us as the "special music" on that particular night, but there we were, in matching dresses, microphones grasped tightly in our fists, singing like there was no tomorrow. Due to the blinding stage lights and consequently not being able to see the expression on people's faces, it was difficult to read how our ministry was being received that night. Dad was the only one positioned in such a way as to be clearly seen. He was beaming!

I was twelve years old when I experienced my most embarrassing moment in regard to being on stage. Dad and I were visiting a church in Minneapolis, Minnesota where he had been invited to preach. As usual, Dad asked me to sing. I agreed, as long as he would sing with me. We practiced and decided to sing one of Dad's favorite hymns, "Wonderful Words of Life." The time came when Dad invited me to join him up front. Guitar in hand, I began making my way toward him. High heels were new to me, and the slippery tile floor between where I was and where my dad was standing, was pitched at a slight incline. I would have made my way to the altar in record time had it not been for the fact my stilted feet slipped from beneath me half way down the aisle! Somehow I managed to hang on to my guitar, but my lanky limbs went flying in all directions. The congregation gasped, I turned ever-deepening shades of red but Dad never batted an eye. He helped me to my feet and accompanied me the rest of what seemed like a *long* way to the front. I've been told that the show went on, and we delivered our song. Personally, I've blocked it out of my memory.

How we did on stage didn't matter so much as far as Dad was concerned. Belonging to him was all that seemed to matter. He loved his kids and got just plain joy out of seeing us up there.

I believe God feels the same way about His kids. He takes great delight in you!

It may be difficult for us to think that God desires to put *His* children on display. Isaiah 61 gives us the proper balance by offering God's perspective:

> *"They will be called oaks of righteousness, a planting of the Lord for the display of His splendor"* (Isaiah 61:3b).

Being on display can be uncomfortable. At times we're tempted to jump off the stage and dive under the nearest pew or give up altogether. What kept Becky going back to the stage was learning where to fix her gaze: on the approving face of her "lawfully proud" Dad. How do we stay on the stage of God's purpose and calling? We fix our eyes on our Heavenly Father, the one who delights in putting us on display for His splendor.

> *"For the Lord takes delight in his people; he crowns the humble with victory."* —Psalm 149:4

When we humbly accept how God desires to display His grace through our lives, we can then faithfully steward what He has given us. Jesus told a parable in Matthew 25:14-30 about a man of means who went on a long journey, entrusting his talents (money) to his servants, each according to his ability. To one he gave five talents, to another two, and to another, one. While the master was away, the servant with five talents immediately put it to work and earned five more. The servant with two did the same, gaining two more. However, the man who had received one talent dug a hole and buried it in the ground. When the master returned, he was pleased with the fruitfulness of the first two servants, but strongly rebuked the third servant saying, "Why did you hide *my* talent in the ground?" The servant responded by saying, "I was afraid and hid *your* talent in the ground." Notice there was no confusion about who owned the treasure! The "talents" God gives us are not ours, *but His*! We are stewards, not owners. They are not about us, but about Him. When we "hide them in the ground," we are hiding Him. When we "put them to work," He gets greater glory. God has given us each a measure of His treasure, each "according to our ability." This may mean standing on a stage or sweeping under the bleachers. How much we have doesn't matter, as much as stewarding well what He has entrusted to us.

Honestly, this parable challenges me (Becky) at a very deep and personal level. Though my sincere prayer and greatest desire has been that God be glorified in and through my life, I've many times expected Him to answer that prayer and fulfill that desire apart from my participation: "Please, Lord, use me, but kindly take me out of the equation!" I was stalled out (again) in this not so humble attitude just a few weeks before beginning to write this book. I began to question God's leading in the project, even though He had been speaking to us about it (and graciously making it abundantly clear) over the previous 5 years. A battle raged in my mind: Did God really have a purpose for these simple stories? What if they failed to reveal the Father's heart, or worse yet left Denver Jones and Becky "front and center" instead of Christ? Horrors!

It was in this place of struggle, I "happened upon" Jesus' parable of the talents. This story was not new to me, but it's message fell on my heart with fresh conviction. I needed to be reminded that these stories were not mine, but His. Further, fear was motivating my desire to hide them, and, as my good husband is fond of saying, "nothing good ever comes from fear."

Maybe you're like me, often dismissing the whispers of the Holy Spirit, mistaking them for my own thoughts. The last time this happened I was challenged by a still small voice, "I haven't called you to be impressive, but obedient." Forgive, me, Lord! The next time you feel a nudge from your Heavenly Father to display His splendor, no matter how simple it seems to you, humbly and obediently release it by faith. When you pray and ask God to do something, it may be He'll ask to do it through you. Keep your gaze on Him and shine. Jesus said, *"Let your light shine before others, that they may see your good deeds and glorify your Father in heaven"* (Matthew 5:16).

Journey to the Father

> "Every faculty you have, your power of thinking or of moving your limbs from moment to moment, is given you by God. If you devoted every moment of your whole life exclusively to His service, you could not give Him anything that was not in a sense His own already."
>
> —C. S. Lewis

Get into the Story:

1. Are you one who is comfortable in the spotlight or runs from it? Why is that?

5: Father's Delight – *"Front and Center"*

2. Consider a time when God placed you "front and center" to do something for Him. How did you respond to the assignment?

_____
_____
_____
_____
_____
_____
_____
_____

3. In your everyday life, how can you pause to see your Heavenly Father's delight as He makes you the *"display of His splendor?"* (Isaiah 61:3b)

_____
_____
_____
_____
_____
_____
_____
_____

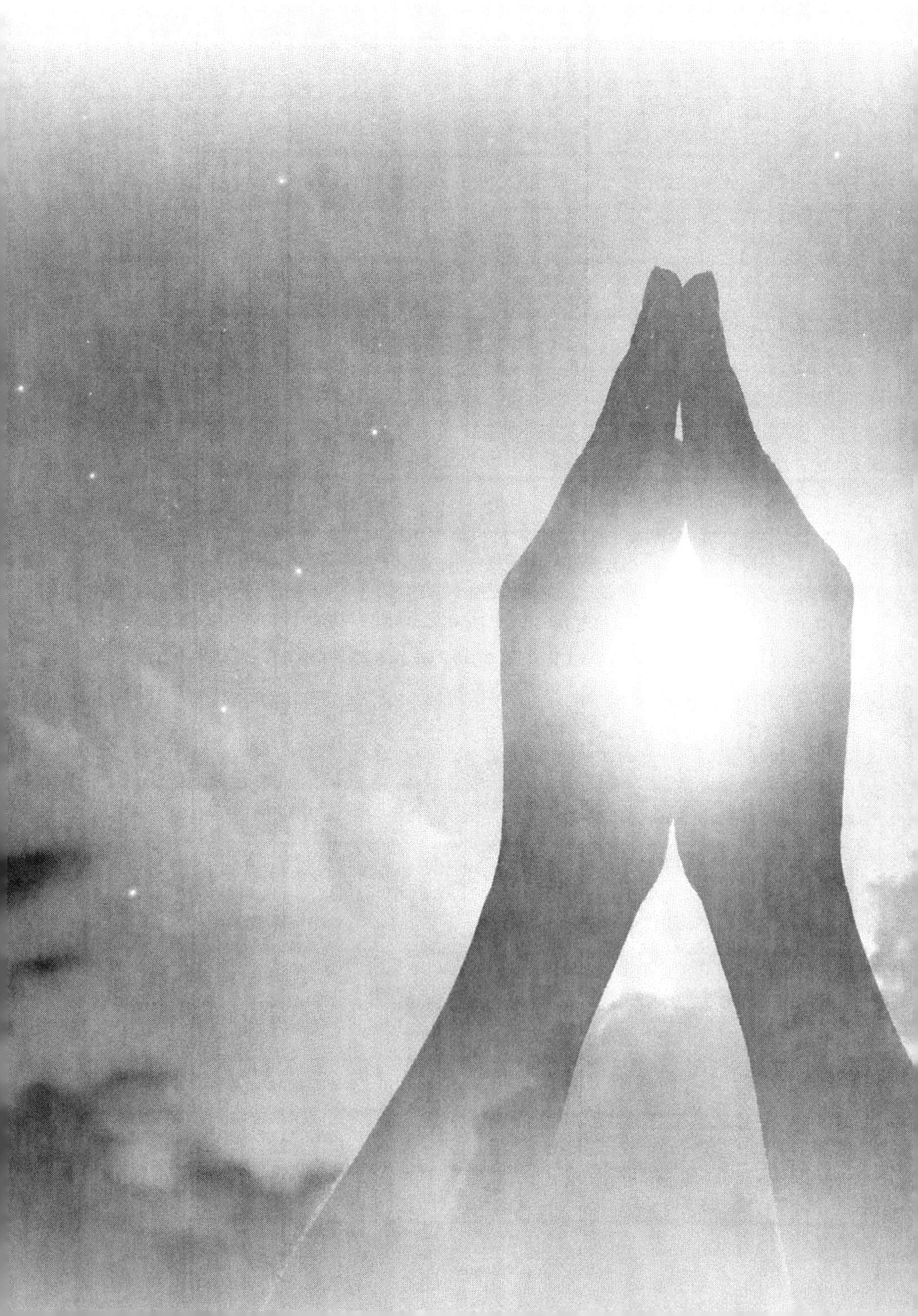

6

Father's Kindness

> "Some people appear to like to have a philanthropic love towards the fallen, but yet they would not touch them with a pair of tongs. They would lift them up if they could, but it must be by some machinery—some sort of contrivance by which they would not degrade themselves or contaminate their own hands. Not so the Savior. Up to the very elbow he seems to thrust that gracious arm of his into the mire, to pull up the lost one out of the horrible pit and out of the miry clay"
>
> —Charles Spurgeon, Sermon: "The Sinner's Friend"

Journey to the Father

Our Father's love for broken people was clearly demonstrated in the life of His Son on earth. In Luke 7:34, Jesus was criticized for being a *"friend of sinners"*. Again, as Jesus was attracting those undesired by the world to him, the religious leaders said, *"This man welcomes sinners and eats with them"* (Luke 15:2). In Luke 19, when Zacchaeus the tax collector gladly welcomed Jesus to his home, *"people began to mutter, 'He has gone to be the guest of a 'sinner.'"* Personally, I am very glad that Jesus bore this title; it gives me hope! He also ate at the home of Pharisees showing that He even welcomes "religious sinners." The Father heart of God is seen in the way Jesus moved *toward* the undesirable of the world.

I wonder if any of us could be accused of being "a friend of sinners." What would it take for people to look at our lives and label us with such a description? In order to be a friend of sinners, we have to go where they are. We have to deliberately place ourselves in their lives. Too often, we Christians only hang out with people who agree with us and act like us. Perhaps we think that by befriending sinners, we might "catch what they've got" and become unholy. How does that emulate our Savior who befriended the most sinful and broken outcasts of society? In reply to the ineffective religious leaders of His day Jesus said, *"It is not the healthy who need a doctor, but the sick. I have not come to call the righteous, but sinners"* (Mark 2:17).

The proclamation of the gospel (good news) was not intended as much for the cavernous, marble halls of cathedrals, as for the hovels, ghettos and backwoods of civilization. This is where the gospel is most effective and does its true work. Jesus even told his disciples, *"The harvest is plentiful, but the workers are few. Ask the Lord of the harvest, therefore, to send out workers into his harvest field. Go! I am sending you out like lambs among wolves"* (Luke 10:2-3). When was the last time you felt like a "lamb" in the midst of "wolves?" This is just the scenario into which Jesus sends us. That sense of vulnerability is not a sign you are in the *wrong place*, but a confirmation that you are in the *right place*: your Father's harvest field!

6: Father's Kindness – "Jesus Goes to Jail"

> "One who has been touched by grace will no longer look on those who stray as 'those evil people' or 'those poor people who need our help.' Nor must we search for signs of 'loveworthiness.' Grace teaches us that God loves because of who God is, not because of who we are."
> —Philip Yancey

Pastor Denver Jones had many "friends" in life. Their degree of sinfulness didn't push him away, but drew him closer. He knew that he was a fellow sinner in desperate need of God's saving grace. That reality moved him toward broken people with compassion and kindness. Further, he did not travel alone, he often had at least one of his kids by his side.

"Jesus Goes to Jail"

I loved going places with dad, as it always guaranteed adventure. I learned much later in life that he had a rather undeveloped sense of direction. The "adventures" we enjoyed so much as kids were the result of his many wrong turns. I don't know that we ever got to where we were going the same way twice. Lets just say we got to regularly explore the roads less travelled. The other perk to going places with Dad was that at some point along the way we would usually stop for some kind of sweet treat. This could have been to stave off hunger (after all, we did spend a considerable time "exploring,") but mostly, we just enjoyed the simple pleasure of it.

On this particular day we ended up on the Main Street in our little town of Grantsburg, Wisconsin. If you're familiar with the 1960's TV classic, *The Andy Griffith Show*, picture Mayberry. After a stop at the local bakery for a "raised glazed" (my favorite donut at the time), we enjoyed a leisurely stroll, admiring the window displays of the charming shops along the way. My hand in his, I looked up and asked, "Dad, where are we going?" "We're going to visit some friends," was his reply.

The Grantsburg County Jail, as it stands in my memory, may as well have been the Mayberry Courthouse. The only difference is that the Sheriff's name wasn't Andy, and he didn't have a deputy named Barney. Stepping inside, I thought the décor, though simple, was pleasant enough. I could tell that the man sitting at the desk with a star-shaped metal badge pinned to his shirt knew my Dad by the way he greeted him. They shook hands and some official looking papers were shuffled and signed. We were then seated across from some men in a little room; the friends we had come to visit, I presumed. I was only five years old at the time, but it seemed curious that these friends sat behind iron bars. Their appearance seemed a little rough, but Dad didn't seem to notice. "Oh well", I reasoned, "any friend of Dad's is a friend of mine."

He greeted these men warmly, asked their names and introduced us both to them. Our visit didn't last too long, but I remember at one point Dad opening the pages of his well-worn Bible, from which he shared a brief message of hope and encouragement. He explained the love and forgiveness available to them through Jesus and prayed for each of them by name.

Dad may have had a poor sense of direction when it came to getting from one place to another, but he sure knew how to point people to Christ.

Jesus is a friend of sinners. I learned that the day Dad and I went to jail.

Being a friend of sinners means that we place ourselves *alongside* people, not *above* them. Here, there is no room for self-justification and looking down on others. *"For all have sinned* and *fall short of the glory of God"* (Romans 3:23). If people detect in us a hyper-religious, holier-than-thou attitude, it puts our relationship with them in jeopardy. We will lose all right to be an influence for God in their life. When unsaved people come into our lives, the first thing they should feel is love; the last thing they should feel from us is judgment. The truth of the gospel is best conveyed through a sincere heart of a close friend.

> *"If you judge people, you have no time to love them."* —Mother Teresa

Being in someone's life doesn't mean we have to agree with his or her direction, lifestyle or worldview. Many Christians think that being with people means that we have to approve of everything about them. This is a snare and will limit your effectiveness and ability to truly becoming a friend of those who need Christ. Jesus sent us with a prayer of protection to represent Him in the world. *"My prayer is not that you take them out of the world but that you protect them from the evil one. They are not of the world, even as I am not of it. Sanctify them by the truth; your word is truth. As you sent me into the world, I have sent them into the world"* (John 17:15-18).

So, the next time you look up at your Heavenly Father and ask, "Where are we going?" don't be surprised if He tells you, "We are going to visit some friends." Take His hand and walk right into the lives of those who need Him most.

Pastor and author Harvey Turner has summarized how we can effectively become "a friend of sinners" in these three helpful points:

1. **Prepare yourself** – pray for courage, the person, yourself.

2. **Be yourself** – God made you uniquely and saved you so that you can be you when doing evangelism.

3. **Forget yourself** – Don't let your self-talk, fear of rejection, and insecurities get in the way of the Gospel. Be more concerned about them and being their friend than you are concerned about how you look or sound. Be present with them.

> "For the Son of Man came to seek and to save what was lost."
> —Luke 19:10

Get into the Story:

1. What would it take for you to be accused of being "a friend of sinners" by an outside observer?

_____

_____

_____

_____

_____

_____

_____

_____

6: Father's Kindness – *"Jesus Goes to Jail"*

2. Who is in the orbit of your life right now that needs Christ? Pray for them and look for an opportunity to share the gospel with them.

3. When was the last time you truly felt compassion for someone in need of grace? Ask the Father to give you His heart for those around you.

7

Father's Discipline

> "We may feel God's hand as a Father upon us when He strikes us as well as when He strokes us." —Abraham Wright

It is common for believers to see our Heavenly Father as always tender, kind, and nurturing. While He certainly possesses these qualities, there is another aspect of our Father's character that is just as real. God, our Father, also disciplines us. That's right; the Bible reveals times when God appropriately brings correction to His children. While some swing too far on the "loving" side of the pendulum in their view of God, thinking He would never discipline His children, others perceive Him as an angry, domineering and dictatorial Father. This image is also far from true according to what we know of Him through Scripture. When He disciplines us, it is always both loving and redemptive in nature.

The clearest biblical text on this subject matter is found in Hebrews chapter 12. The truths laid out here give us a sound and balanced understanding of our Father's discipline. While we live in an age when the whole idea of child discipline is being questioned, valuable and timeless principles for our own parenting can be found here. Lets look at this passage section-by-section and draw out some helpful observations from Hebrews 12:4-11

v. 4-5a *"In your struggle against sin, you have not yet resisted to the point of shedding your blood. And have you completely forgotten this word of encouragement that addresses you as a father addresses his son?"* - Notice that the writer of Hebrews opens the topic of our Father's discipline by calling it a *"word of encouragement!"* The very fact that we undergo divine discipline is proof that we are in a Father/child relationship with God. Be encouraged!

v. 5b-6 *"My son, do not make light of the Lord's discipline, and do not lose heart when he rebukes you because the Lord disciplines the one he loves, and he chastens everyone he accepts as his son."* - We see here two inappropriate responses to discipline: 1) to make light of it, or 2) to lose heart. Both of these emotional reactions reveal that we have missed the point entirely. Discipline is one way a good parent displays love for their child...it is the same with our Father. Verse six, above, makes it clear, if you are a *"son,"* (or daughter) you will be *"chastened."*

v. 7-8 *"Endure hardship as discipline; God is treating you as his children. For what children are not disciplined by their father? If you are not disciplined—and everyone undergoes discipline—then you are not legitimate, not true sons and daughters at all."* - It may seem strange to view the various "hardships" that touch our lives as discipline. Our Father can and will use a full array of means to touch our hearts and redirect our lives. He may employ natural circumstances, other people, physical challenges, financial issues, or deep inner sorrow over sin. Everything that enters our lives comes through our Father's full and sovereign knowledge. We need not obsess over the source of our trouble or why we are suffering hardship as much as considering carefully our response to it.

7: Father's Discipline – "The Chicken Coop Confession"

v. 9-10 *"Moreover, we have all had human fathers who disciplined us and we respected them for it. How much more should we submit to the Father of spirits and live! They disciplined us for a little while as they thought best; but God disciplines us for our good, in order that we may share in his holiness."* - This section rightly compares our natural father's discipline with that of our Heavenly Father. Proper parental discipline is a *"respectable"* act and is clearly *"for our good."* Our best response to God's correction is to *"submit to it... and live."* This is the way He enables us to *"share in His holiness."*

v. 11 *"No discipline seems pleasant at the time, but painful. Later on, however, it produces a harvest of righteousness and peace for those who have been trained by it."* - Once, after spanking one of our children, she defiantly replied, "Oh, that didn't hurt." We will let you guess how we responded to that! The fact is, discipline should hurt...even God's discipline. It is not *"pleasant at the time, but painful."* Pain has a way of getting our attention like nothing else! Notice the powerful phrase, *"for those who have been trained by it."* There is a big difference between going through the pain of discipline and being *trained* by the pain of discipline. The latter produces in us a *"harvest of righteousness and peace."*

> "We want not so much a father in heaven as a grandfather in heaven... whose plan for the universe was simply that it might be truly said at the end of each day, 'a good time was had by all'" —C. S. Lewis

Pastor Denver Jones loved all of his children enough to discipline them. He realized early on that there wasn't a "one size fits all" approach. Each of their unique temperaments informed what method and measure of correction was appropriate for a given offense. No parent takes delight when his or her child misbehaves or the moments of discipline that follow. The common parental phrase "This is going to hurt me more than it hurts you."

is often more of a truth than an empty adage. Such was the case for Denver as he parented his young, sometimes rambunctious daughter, Becky.

"The Chicken Coop Confession"

There was a twinge of "something about this might not be wise" the day my friend and I decided to use the windows of a seemingly useless shack as targets for rock-throwing practice. On the other hand, it seemed the old building served no other purpose than to hold junk. The pleasure gained from the delightful sound of shattering glass and the satisfaction of hitting a relatively small target from an impressive distance outweighed any momentary hesitation. Both caution and rocks were thrown to the wind, resulting in major damage to what I found out later was our neighbor's chicken coop!

A few days later my Dad posed this simple question to my sisters and me... "Girls, do you know who broke the chicken coop windows?" The answer was simple for two out of three of us. Mary?, He asked. No. Pat? No. Becky?... Becky...?

The answer should have been simple for me too. In a word, it would have been, "Yes," But sometimes the simple truth seems so complicated. The truth was, I knew EVERYTHING about said windows. But *telling* the truth? It was complicated for sure and potentially painful!

My dad proceeded by personalizing the question, "Becky, do you know anything about the chicken coop windows?" Shifting my glance from Dad's eyes to my shoes, I hesitated and then sheepishly indicated my reply by shaking my head, no.

I was stunned when Dad gently but firmly responded to my lie, "Becky, please go to my room and wait for me there." It was then I learned that no matter how complicated telling the truth seems, lying always complicates things further!

With a heavy heart I made the short journey from the driveway to Dad's room, strangely long and tortuous that particular day.

There I waited in the quiet, a flurry of questions racing through my mind. Did Dad know what happened? (Turns out my friend and accomplice in crime told the truth to her dad when confronted.) If he knew the truth, why didn't he just tell me outright? What kind of punishment awaited me?

The window-breaking incident, by a stretch, could be classified as childish irresponsibility, but a blatant lie? There was no reasonable defense.

The look on my Dad's face as he awaited my confession that day is something I'll never forget. It crushed me. I knew I had deeply disappointed him. The guilt of broken windows paled in comparison to the grief of a damaged relationship.

My confession was not long in forthcoming. I can imagine dad studying my response and praying for wisdom to discern the appropriate disciplinary action. He must have seen genuine repentance at work in my heart, because instead of delivering a well deserved spanking, he accepted my sincere apology and granted forgiveness, no strings attached. This certainly wasn't the last time I needed discipline, but as far as I can remember, it is the last time I lied to my dad.

Confession is good for the soul after all.

Becky's dad, Denver, had full knowledge of her guilt in the case of the chicken coop windows. He could have pointed out her sin, rightfully condemned and punished her, case closed. Instead, he invited her confession and graciously offered forgiveness. "Coming clean" was more for her benefit than his. It was the only way for her to off-load the heavy burden of guilt and shame. It is that way with our Heavenly Father. *"If we confess our sins, he is faithful and just and will forgive our sins and purify us from all unrighteousness"* (1 John 1:9).

Becky's halting childhood confession reminds us of the many times we stand in need of forgiveness before our Heavenly Father; eyes downcast, beholding our "shoes of condemnation" rather than Jesus' gaze of compassion. Romans 8:1 tells us, *"There is now no condemnation for those who are in Christ Jesus."* Amazing isn't it? Condemnation has no place in our Father's discipline. His correction is not vague, leaving us to stand continually under a dark and heavy cloud of general unworthiness, but specific, inviting repentance unto an immediate standing of freedom. Our enemy uses condemnation to turn us *away from* the Father. Conviction is a gift of the Holy Spirit that that prompts us to run *toward* the Father.

When repentance is sincere, forgiveness is complete. We are assured of this in Psalm 103:11-13, *"For as high as the heavens are above the earth, so great is his love for those who fear him; as far as the east is from the west, so far has he removed our transgressions from us. As a father has compassion on his children, so the Lord has compassion on those who fear him."* We can be confused on this point if we don't understand that God's *forgiveness* of our sin is something completely different than the natural *consequences* of our sin. Even when we have received complete forgiveness for a particular sin, we may still have some very practical consequences to walk through on our way out of the mess we created. As we respond properly to His loving discipline, we can be assured that God will never raise the offense again.

Several years ago we had the privilege of ministering at a great church in Hamilton, New Zealand. Posted in their prayer room was this intriguing

7: Father's Discipline – "The Chicken Coop Confession"

message, "Maybe, just maybe, Jesus is nicer than you think He is." How often do we consider the Son of God in terms of "niceness?" Romans 2:4 reads, *""Or do you show contempt for the riches of his kindness, forbearance and patience, not realizing that God's kindness is intended to lead you to repentance?"* Do you have a hard time wrapping your mind around this? Imagine if your child had disobeyed and was in rebellion. Most of us would be inclined to dole out kindness only *after* they had apologized and shaped up not *before!* Next time we pray for someone who has spiritually lost their way, dare we ask God to chase them down with His kindness?

As we mature, we realize that the true pain of sin is not only in our wrongdoing, but in the breaking of our Father's heart. When wrestling with sin of any kind; lust, gossip, greed, fear, etc., we often fight to avoid them because we know instinctively that they are morally wrong, bad for us, or harmful to our relationships. When convicted about doing wrong, we feel sad, grieved, and mad at ourselves. However, all this anguish around our sinful actions misses a bigger point. Our Father knows fully when we walk into sin - willfully or unintentionally - and it breaks His heart. This may not jeopardize our standing as His children, but it does affect the close fellowship we have with our loving Lord. His greatest delight is when we live fully and vitally in unbroken communion with Him. Knowing this, Satan works overtime - not simply to get us doing "bad things," but to hinder the openness and freedom we enjoy with our Father. This was the serpent's strategy in the Garden of Eden, which he repeats today. Sin, being much more than an affront to God's holiness, denies our identity as His image-bearers.

> *"But if we walk in the light, as he is in the light, we have fellowship with one another, and the blood of Jesus, his Son, purifies us from all sin."* —1 John 1:7

Journey to the Father

So, the next time God asks you, "Do you know anything about the chicken coop windows?" run *toward* Him, not *away* from Him. Freely and fully confess your sin and receive His complete forgiveness, no strings attached. He is a forgiving and restorative Father!

Get into the Story:

1. Did your natural parents' discipline set you up to properly understand the discipline of your Heavenly Father? If necessary, ask the Holy Sprit to adjust your perspective, beliefs and attitudes according to what is true of Him.

_____
_____
_____
_____
_____
_____
_____
_____

7: Father's Discipline – *"The Chicken Coop Confession"*

2. Of the two wrong responses to divine discipline given in Hebrews 12:5 (make light of it or lose heart), which one tends to be your most common reaction? What can you do to improve your response to God?

3. How can seeing sin as "breaking God's heart" keep you from going astray?

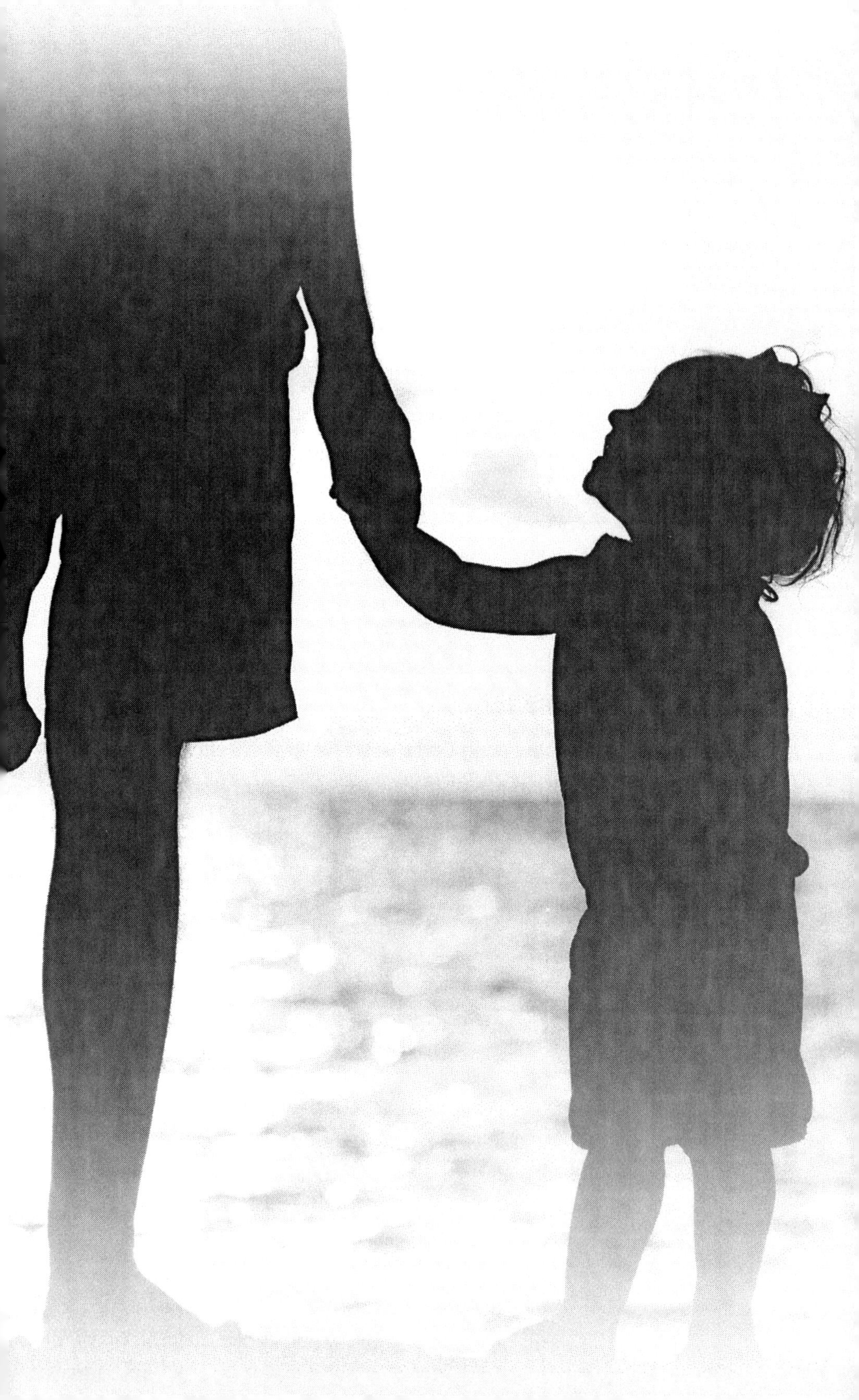

8

Father's Presence

> "God's presence is not the same as the feeling of God's presence and He may be doing most for us when we think He is doing least."
>
> —C. S. Lewis

Perhaps one of the greatest blessings we have as children of God is the promise of our Father's presence. It banishes our fears, settles our insecurities, and transforms our weaknesses into strengths. Knowing He is near allows us to move in confidence and authority. If our Father is with us, we feel nothing is impossible. King David wrote of such confidence in Psalm 18:29, *"With your help I can advance against a troop; with my God I can scale a wall."* Conversely, when we lose a sense of His presence, our faith is shaken. When King David was pleading for God's forgiveness after his sins of adultery and murder, his concern for God's presence was forefront in his mind. He writes, *"Create in me a pure heart, O God, and renew a steadfast spirit within me. Do not cast me from your presence or take your Holy Spirit from me"* (Psalm 51:10-11). Amid all the anguish David experienced in recovering from his sin, the thing he longed for most was the awareness of God's presence.

If we are going to be our Father's ambassadors, effectively representing His kingdom on earth, we must hold this firm conviction: wherever we go, He goes with us. At times, we can lose sight of this reality. The concept of God's presence can seem mystical and hard to grasp. Perhaps these three aspects of our Father's presence can bring some clarity:

> **1) God's Promised Presence** – Because our Father is omnipresent - present at all times and places - we can be assured that He is with us continually. (Psalm 139:7-10; Jeremiah 23:24; Matthew 28:20)
>
> **2) God's Manifest Presence** – There are times when the Lord's presence breaks into our natural world in a supernatural display of His glory. (Luke 5:17; Acts 4:8; 9:5; I Corinthians 14:25)
>
> **3) God's Ultimate Presence** – When Christ returns or we see Him in heaven, we will be in the fullness of His presence. (John 17:24; John 14:3; I John 3:2)

One could say that we *live* in God's Promised Presence, *visit* God's Manifest Presence and *look forward to* God's Ultimate Presence. When Jesus commissioned us to go to the ends of the earth with the gospel, He gave us a great promise, *"Surely I am with you always, to the very end of the age"* (Matthew 28:20).

There are times in our ministry we find ourselves in a far off country facing a challenging spiritual environment. It is easy to let our minds protest, "How did you get yourself into this situation and what are you going to do now that you're here?" God is so faithful to make His presence known. There have been times when I (Sonny) have physically felt a hand on my shoulder bringing me comfort and assurance. What a thrill when God's promised presence becomes His manifest presence. It creates an even deeper longing for His ultimate presence.

8: Father's Presence – *"A Pillar of Hope"*

> "I must first have the sense of God's possession of me before I can have the sense of His presence with me." —Watchman Nee

As we live our lives by faith, there are times we need confirmation that our Father is with us and is guiding our steps. Even the great Apostle Paul needed this assurance while planting the church in Corinth. *"One night the Lord spoke to Paul in a vision: "Do not be afraid; keep on speaking, do not be silent. For I am with you, and no one is going to attack and harm you, because I have many people in this city"* (Acts 18:9-10). Again, when Paul was being taken as a prisoner to Rome, the ship he was on sailed right into a vicious Mediterranean storm. After fourteen days of being battered, all on board feared for their lives. Then Paul stood to say, *"Last night an angel of the God to whom I belong and whom I serve stood beside me and said, 'Do not be afraid, Paul. You must stand trial before Caesar; and God has graciously given you the lives of all who sail with you'"* (Acts 27:23-24). Wasn't our Father gracious to have this message of His presence and protection personally delivered? He knows how to confirm His presence when we need it.

Becky's dad, Denver, and his family moved to Stewartville, Minnesota in the summer of 1971. Just as they began settling in, their life became quickly and dramatically unsettled. Among other difficult circumstances beyond their control, Becky's mother, Dorothy, found out her cancer had returned. Consequently, Becky faced the first day of a new school year with plenty of insecurity. Through this fearful experience, she learned a timeless lesson from her dad: the power of our Father's promised presence.

"A Pillar of Hope"

Life can suddenly feel as though the ground has opened up beneath us. In order to avoid being swallowed, we cling in fear to the closest seeming-solid thing. My solid thing happened to be a pillar on the front porch of our home. The house was originally designed and operated as a nursing home, but had long since been used as a private residence. A dear Christian friend made it available to us since it was ideal for the ministry dream God had given my parents: a church plant and the establishment of a Bible-training center in Stewartville, Minnesota.

It was late summer, 1971, when my family made the bold and radical move from our cozy farmhouse in Wisconsin to this three-story "mansion" in Minnesota. The young couple that originally had the vision to start this new work, The Restoration Ministry Center, would occupy the third floor, our family would reside on the second floor, and the main floor would house the Ministry Center.

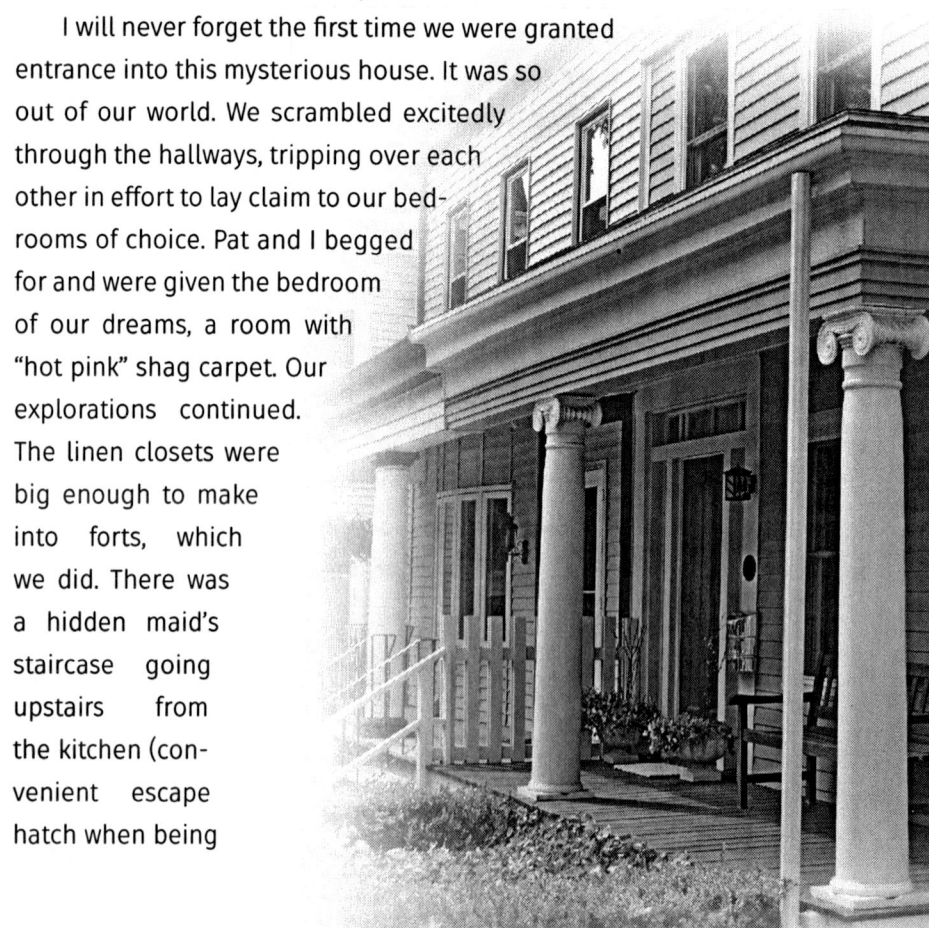

I will never forget the first time we were granted entrance into this mysterious house. It was so out of our world. We scrambled excitedly through the hallways, tripping over each other in effort to lay claim to our bedrooms of choice. Pat and I begged for and were given the bedroom of our dreams, a room with "hot pink" shag carpet. Our explorations continued. The linen closets were big enough to make into forts, which we did. There was a hidden maid's staircase going upstairs from the kitchen (convenient escape hatch when being beckoned for chores), a winding main staircase with a banister perfect for sliding down (which we did when no one was looking), and a laundry chute (which ideally facilitated the transference of secret spy intelligence). We children immediately saw the potential in this house for great adventure. The house also featured a large gathering room (former nursing home dining hall), large kitchen, and plenty of restrooms – a Ministry Center just waiting to happen. We moved in with conflicting emotions, aching over the life and loved ones we'd left behind, and yet trying our best to be hopeful for what lay ahead.

It took heaven's perspective to fully understand the confusing why's of our three years in that place. The ministry dream that propelled our move now left us sorely disappointed. Further, shortly after we settled in mom's cancer returned with a vengeance. By spring, we were rattling around in the big house, and she was at home in heaven.

But let's back up that fall and the front porch pillar onto which I clung for dear life. It was the first day of school, and I had made the decision not to go. I would spend my second grade year at home campaigning for no more change! The amber flashing lights of the approaching school bus came into view. The urging of my siblings to join them as they boarded only deepened my resolve. They stalled the driver as long as they were able, until finally the bus slowly pulled away. Victory at last! Second grade would forever remain in my rear-view mirror.

Dad was nearby when my grip on my own false reality began to loosen. I am hard pressed to know how I would have responded if I were in his shoes. He could have tried the strong-arm, "life is hard, get over it" approach, or bargaining (unmerited candy usually went a long way in buying my compliance). He could have given in and said, "You're right, this is too hard. Why don't you stay home, and we'll see how you feel tomorrow." I think he identified with my fears and sense of vulnerability. With all the heartache of this season, he was likely tempted to call it quits, dropping out of his own school of hard-knocks. But instead, he spoke 5 simple and powerful words, which linger in my heart to this day. He said tenderly, "I will go with you."

Hmmm, I hadn't thought of that. It struck me as the perfect solution. We drove to school and found my classroom. Dad and I made friends with my new teacher and some of the other kids. Before long, I was settled in and waving goodbye to Dad.

It's amazing what you can face when your dad goes with you!

Our Father does not send us anywhere alone. His Holy Spirit is with us, upon us, and in us. He empowers us to bring His glory to the world. When we launch out— whether it is to start 2nd grade, a new job or a new marriage, visit a neighbor across the street, or to head off to a foreign mission field— we can be assured of His presence.

God had a unique way of demonstrating His presence to the fledgling Hebrew nation as they were coming out of Egypt and traversing the great wilderness. *"By day the Lord went ahead of them in a pillar of cloud to guide them on their way and by night in a pillar of fire to give them light, so that they could travel by day or night"* Exodus 13:21. *"The pillar of cloud also moved from in front and stood behind them, coming between the armies of Egypt and Israel"* (Exodus 14:19b-20a). The pillar went ahead of God's people, providing clear and continual guidance. It moved behind them, providing supernatural protection. His presence provides the same for us today!

Later, when God determined not to go with them because they were a stiff-necked people, Moses interceded by reminding the Lord that His unique presence with them was the distinguishing mark upon His people. We see this story in Exodus 33: *"When the people heard these distressing words, they began to mourn and no one put on any ornaments. For the Lord had said to Moses, "Tell the Israelites, 'You are a stiff-necked people. If I were to go with you even for a moment, I might destroy you.' ...Then Moses said to him, 'If your Presence does not go with us, do not send us up from here. How will anyone know that you are pleased with me and with your people unless you go with us? What else will distinguish me and your people from all the other people on the face of the earth?'"* (Exodus 33:4-5, 15-16).

As the Israelites were preparing to enter the Promised Land, God spoke to their leader, Joshua, instructing him to proceed with confidence, free of fear, and discouragement. *"Have I not commanded you? Be strong and courageous. Do not be afraid; do not be discouraged, for the Lord your God will be with you wherever you go"* (Joshua 1:9).

The next time you find yourself in a place of fear and insecurity, cling to the One who promises to go with you. Then go forward in the confidence His presence provides.

> "So do not fear, for I am with you; do not be dismayed, for I am your God. I will strengthen you and help you; I will uphold you with my righteous right hand." —Isaiah 41:10

Journey to the Father

Get into the Story:

1. When you lack confidence in God's presence, what "pillars" of false security are you tempted to hold on to?

2. Describe a time when God's "promised presence" became His "manifest presence"? How did this strengthen your faith?

3. What practices have helped you regain your sense of God's presence? (solitude, worship, reading Scripture, fasting, praying with friends, serving others, being in nature)

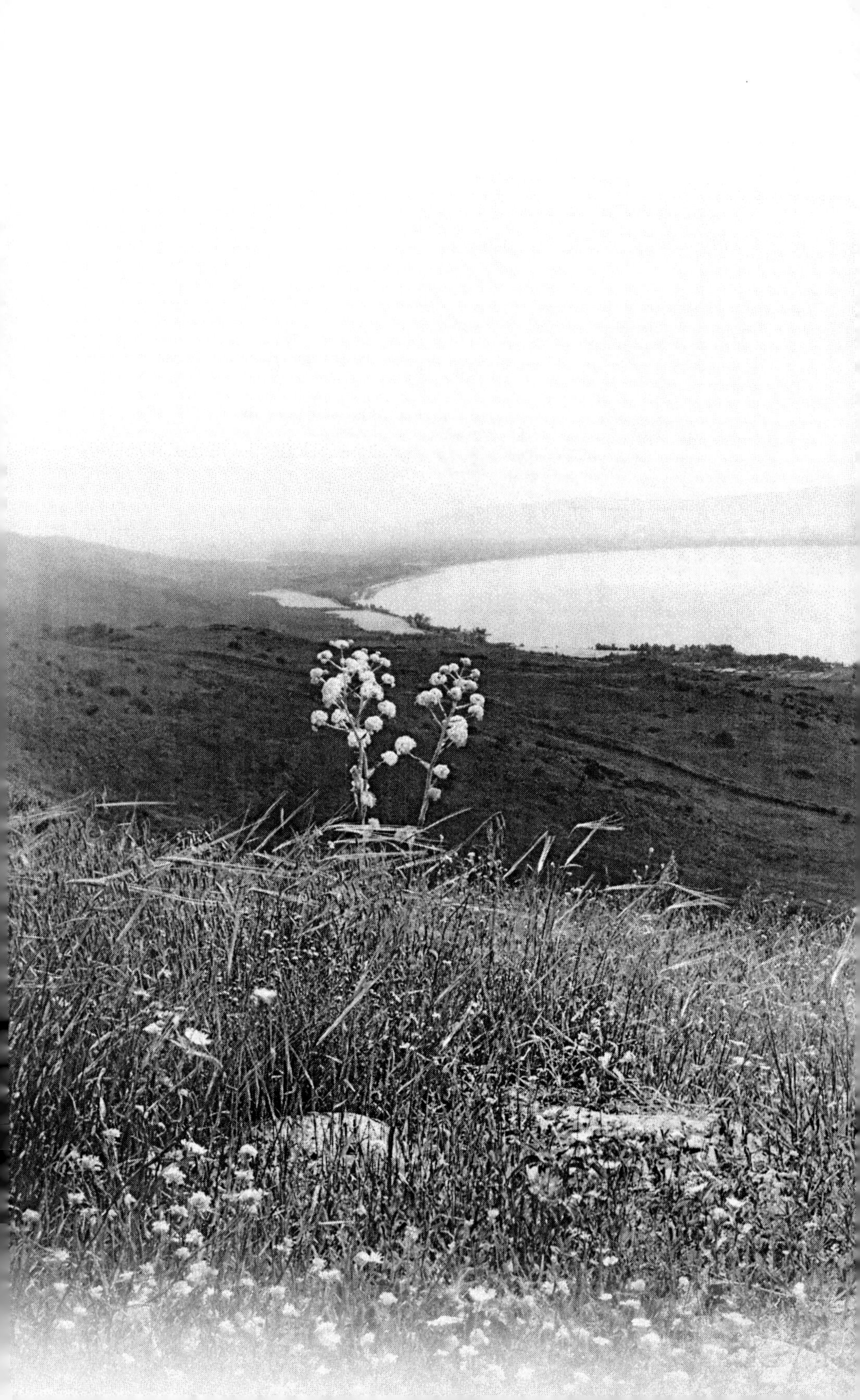

9

Father's Provision

> "It is a safe thing to trust Him to fulfill the desires which He creates."
> —Amy Carmichael

"Do not worry...for your Heavenly Father knows..." This is the essence of Jesus' message as He addressed a large crowd of followers one day on the side of a mountain on the northern shores of the Sea of Galilee. Let's seat ourselves among the crowd, lean in, and listen closely to Jesus comforting, yet challenging words:

"Therefore I tell you, do not worry about your life, what you will eat or drink; or about your body, what you will wear. Is not life more than food, and the body more than clothes? Look at the birds of the air; they do not sow or reap or store away in barns, and yet your heavenly Father feeds them. Are you not much more valuable than they? Can any one of you by worrying add a single hour to your life? And why do you worry about clothes? See how the

flowers of the field grow. They do not labor or spin. Yet I tell you that not even Solomon in all his splendor was dressed like one of these. If that is how God clothes the grass of the field, which is here today and tomorrow is thrown into the fire, will he not much more clothe you—you of little faith? So do not worry, saying, 'What shall we eat?' or 'What shall we drink?' or 'What shall we wear?' For the pagans run after all these things, and your heavenly Father knows that you need them. But seek first his kingdom and his righteousness, and all these things will be given to you as well" (Matthew 6:25-33).

Do not worry. Is that a suggestion, command, or even possible? Some of us act as though worry is our right and responsibility and make it a full-time job! Yet, Jesus gives us an alternative to a life-style of anxiety. Trust His care and provision. Seek Him and His righteousness *first*. We are in greater need of the *Giver* than His gifts, but He graciously gives them as well.

Before they left the hillside that day, Jesus has something equally amazing to teach them about prayer: *"And when you pray, do not keep on babbling like pagans, for they think they will be heard because of their many words. Do not be like them, for your Father knows what you need before you ask him"* (Matthew 6:7-8). Jesus tells us that our best prayers are not necessarily our longest prayers. Longwinded diatribes don't impress Him. In fact, our observation is that the most sincere prayers tend to be the shortest. Jesus also said that our Father knows what we need even *before* we ask. Amazingly, our wise Father knows the intimate details of our life and is aware of our concern over a needed job, an important decision that has to be made, and our longing to see a wayward child turn back to Christ. Because of this, our faith can be simple and our words few.

When we face a crisis and seek His direction, our natural mind tends to think of the two best solutions to present to God as His options; He must really smile at us sometimes! While it is noble for us to seek solutions to our problems, our perspective is limited. Our wonderful "Option #1" and our clever "Option #2" actually fall far short of the blessing God really has in store. Our Father is the God of the Third *and best* Option. If we wait for His answer, we will see just how wise and generous He is. The Apostle Paul's prayer reflects this when he says, *"Now to him who is able to do immeasurably more than all we ask or imagine, according to his power that is at work within us"* (Ephesians 3:20).

Often, the greatest miracles are realized in seasons of greatest need. This was the case for Denver and Dorothy Jones as they were raising their five children on a church-planter's budget. For them, the Father was truly the Giver of good gifts!

"Gifts Unforeseen"

Many years have passed since the Christmas of 1971. I was only 7 years old, but the memories of that miraculous December remain vivid in my mind. My family didn't know it at the time, but this would be our last Christmas with Mom on this side of heaven. She was battling breast cancer. The image of our strong and vibrant Mother was quickly fading into the new normal of hearing her moan in pain as she lay in the hospital bed that now occupied space in my parent's bedroom. It had been weeks since she'd had strength to rise from her bed of affliction.

Mom was the undisputed leader when it came to organizing and implementing family events. This Christmas, Dad was clearly out of his element. Our little sister Jodi was only 16 months old and thusly pardoned from any responsibility beyond cuteness. The remaining four of us kids, who at that time ranged in age from seven to fourteen, formed a decent decorating crew and saw to it that we at least had a Christmas tree with lights and tinsel.

The thing that troubled Dad the most was the lack of gifts under the tree. There was simply no money for presents that year. He was used to approaching the throne of grace for provision. "Give us this day our daily bread" was not a rote recitation in our family, but an earnest and sincere daily prayer. In this instance, however, Dad's deep desire never surfaced as a prayer - at least not one with words.

Evidently, words are not always necessary, because a few days before Christmas, Dad's wordless prayer was answered in a big way. A friend came to the house unexpectedly and placed an envelope into Dad's hand. "Denver," said this kind and generous man, "I want you to have this money for the sole purpose of providing Christmas presents for your family." This gentleman left as quickly as he came, leaving Dad standing at the door, stunned and thankful beyond words. Overnight, the scene in our living room changed from languishing to lavishing. Not only were there gifts under the tree, they were stacked up like towers on both sides. Imagine the joy this brought to my Dad and Mom's heart, not to mention the elation we felt as children.

Christmas Eve arrived to our soaring expectation. It was a magical night and began at the table with the best gift of all; Mom found the strength to leave her bed, get dressed, and descend the long flight of stairs from her bedroom to our dining room. This seemed no less than miraculous.

We gathered around our candlelit table, eyes filled with wonder and hearts brimming with joy. Our family circle was complete as we joined hands to pray. While I was sincerely thankful, I could hardly wait for the "amen" to be said. It was time to eat, and our extravagant fare consisted of TV dinners and red punch. This was the ultimate in fine dining! Brought up on Mom's delicious homemade cooking, there was something novel about a TV dinner with each part sectioned out and neatly arranged in its tinfoil tray. Besides that, we had been given the privilege and pleasure of choosing our meal from all the wonderful varieties in the freezer department of the grocery store. In our minds, it didn't get any better than this!

After our special meal, it was time for what had become a Jones household tradition: a live dramatization of the Christmas story. We scrambled through the house pulling together simple props, including the dishtowels we wore as head coverings, until we successfully created our version of the manger scene. An otherwise ordinary doll

9: Father's Provision – *"Gifts Unforeseen"*

unearthed from the bottom of the toy box became Baby Jesus and was tucked tenderly inside Mary's bathrobe. A holy hush fell over the living room as Mary and Joseph began their long and arduous journey to Bethlehem. The culminating scene found us all on our knees before the babe (who had been successfully delivered and laid in the manger), singing with all the awe and gusto of a heavenly host, "Oh come let us adore Him..." Although the heartfelt performance by us children lacked Broadway class, it was met with an enthusiastic response from our adoring fans, otherwise known as Mom and Dad.

This particular year, just as the "heavenly hosts" were bringing the last chorus of "O Come All Ye Faithful" in for a landing, our sacred drama took a surprising twist. For, in came Santa Clause, singing his own merry chorus of "Ho, ho, ho," and bearing gifts for each of us! Considering his timing it seemed safe to assume God had sent him. (It was later revealed our neighbor had.)

Just when we thought it couldn't get any more exciting, it was announced that the time had come to open our family Christmas presents.

There were more gifts that year than any other before or since. I specifically recall two of the gifts I received that Christmas Eve. One was a doll named "Drowsy," which spoke phrases like, "I want another drink of water," and "I'm sleepy," and "I love you," with each pull of her string. The other was a classical guitar. My two older sisters, Mary and Pat, each received one as well. The significance of my guitar deserves a story of its own, but for now I'll tell you that it became cherished, and well used. It is still making beautiful music to this day.

Our Heavenly Father is a generous gift giver. This truth is most powerfully demonstrated in times of our greatest need, just as our family experienced that miraculous Christmas of 1971.

> "Every good and perfect gift is from above, coming down from the Father of the heavenly lights, who does not change like shifting shadows." — James 1:17

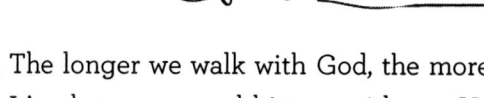

The longer we walk with God, the more we know Him to be trustworthy. It's what a personal history with our Heavenly Father teaches us. It's not because we always get from Him what we ask for; but that we come to understand He knows and loves us. Our faith is sure because He is faithful. James Hudson Taylor was a groundbreaking missionary to China in the mid to late 1800's. Having served the Chinese people for 51 years, he is credited with bringing over 800 missionaries into that great land. In a letter written to his wife during a particularly trying time with the mission, Taylor reported, "We have twenty-five cents – and all the promises of God!" Hudson knew that he needed no more.

> The Lord is my shepherd, I lack nothing. – Psalm 23:1-3

If you find yourself in a place of desperate need, bring your concern to your Heavenly Father then leave it fully in His care. Even though he knows what

9: Father's Provision – *"Gifts Unforeseen"*

we need before we ask, He still wants us to come to Him in prayer. Prayer is an exercise in intimacy and abject dependence. This is the kind of faith that pleases God. Matthew 7:7-11 says, *"Ask, seek, knock...if you, then, though you are evil, know how to give good gifts to your children, how much more will your Father in heaven give good gifts to those who ask."*

> *If you have a special need today, focus your full attention on the goodness and greatness of your Father rather than on the size of your need. Your need is tiny compared to His ability to meet it.* —Bill Patterson

Get into the Story:

1. Consider a time when you were in need, but powerless to change your situation. How did you respond?

2. Has there ever been a time when you laid out all your natural options to God only to discover that He was "the God of the third option?" How did His option change the outcome?

3. Take time to express in writing your thanks to God for His practical provision for you. Praise Him for how He uses people and circumstances to demonstrate His faithfulness. With this great hymn, consider freshly entrusting every burden to your generous Heavenly Father's care:

9: Father's Provision – *"Gifts Unforeseen"*

He Giveth More Grace

by Annie J Flint

He giveth more grace when the burdens grow greater,
He sendeth more strength when the labors increase;
To added afflictions He addeth His mercy,
To multiplied trials, His multiplied peace.

When we have exhausted our store of endurance,
When our strength has failed ere the day is half done,
When we reach the end of our hoarded resources
Our Father's full giving is only begun.

Chorus:

His love has no limit, His grace has no measure,
His power has no boundary known unto men;
For out of His infinite riches in Jesus
He giveth, and giveth, and giveth again.

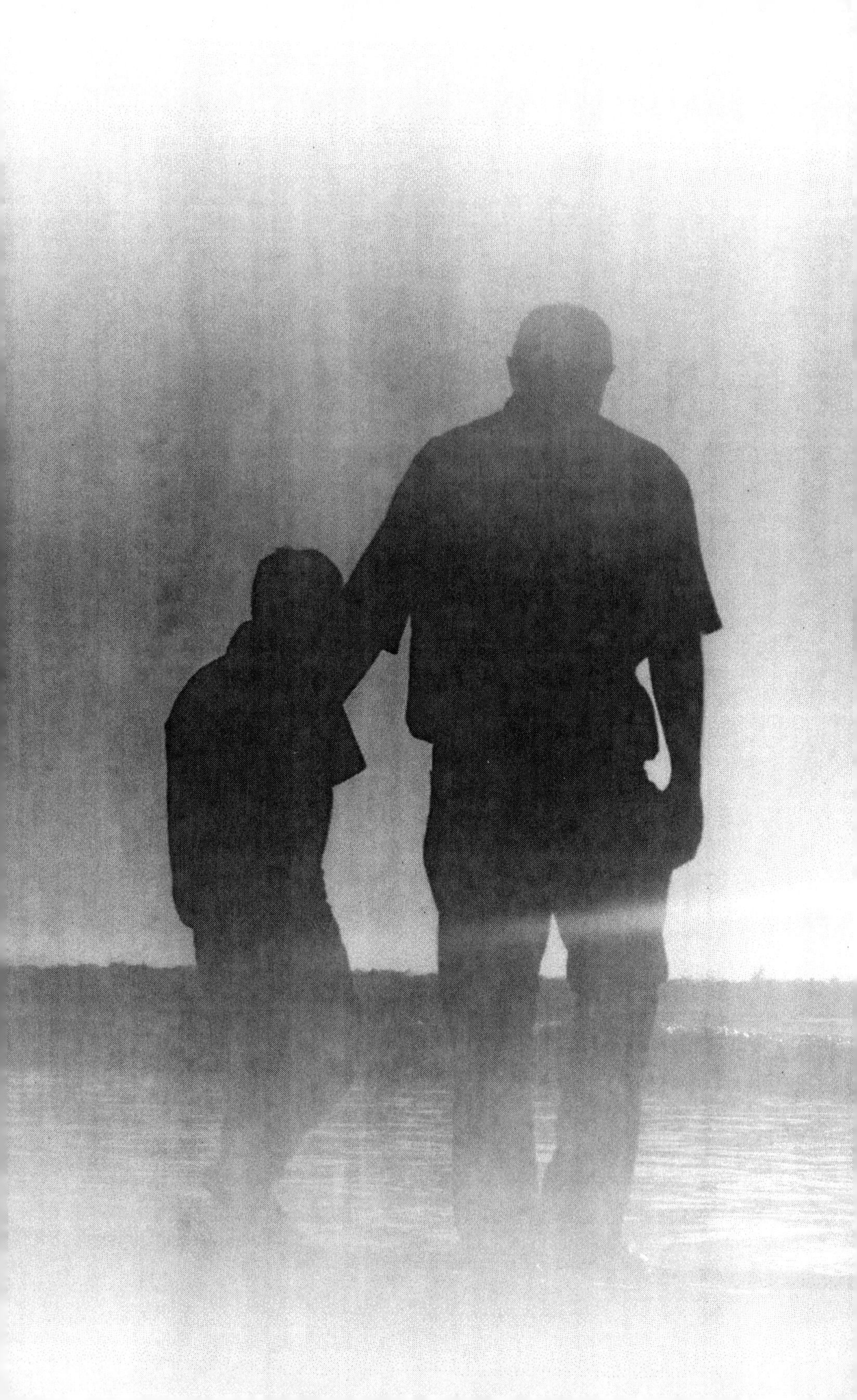

10

Father's Comfort

> *"The death of a beloved is an amputation."* —C.S. Lewis

Nothing seemed fair about Dorothy Jones being taken from her husband and five children at the young age of 42. The cancer had returned, and her bravely fought nine-month battle was now over. Her husband, Denver, who stood in faith with her for healing, was heartbroken. First, there was disbelief, then pain, so much deep pain. How would he care for his family? Would the struggling church plant die as well? How does a pastor grieve – one who spends so much time helping others through their own pain? Who shares the Scriptures of hope with him? Would they even mean much to him in this dark hour? The Jones children cling to one another in their anguish; they cling to their Dad. Why weren't their prayers for Mom's healing answered? Doesn't God honor child-like faith? Now she is gone, and what are they to do? Grief brings a profound insecurity.

Our Heavenly Father speaks much through His word to help us in our grief. David, the blessed psalmist, wrote from his own experience, *"The LORD is close to the brokenhearted and saves those who are crushed in spirit"* (Psalm 34:18). Isaiah the prophet, when describing the Messiah to come, said He would be *"a man of suffering, and familiar with pain"* (Isaiah 53:3). Jesus brings assurance in His great Sermon on the Mount, *"Blessed are those who mourn, for they will be comforted"* (Matthew 5:4). The Apostle Paul tells us that God makes an investment in us when we receive His comfort. He enables us to draw on this investment uniquely when helping others. *"Praise be to the God and Father of our Lord Jesus Christ, the Father of compassion and the God of all comfort, who comforts us in all our troubles, so that we can comfort those in any trouble with the comfort we ourselves receive from God"* (II Corinthians 1:3-4). And at the end of the ages, we are given this great promise: *"And I heard a loud voice from the throne saying, 'Look! God's dwelling place is now among the people, and he will dwell with them. They will be his people, and God himself will be with them and be their God. 'He will wipe every tear from their eyes. There will be no more death' or mourning or crying or pain, for the old order of things has passed away"* (Revelation 21:3-4).

> "Suffering is meaningful. There is a purpose to it, and if faced rightly, it can drive us like a nail deep into the love of God and into more stability and spiritual power than you can imagine." —Tim Keller

In a very tangible way, God used their earthly father to bring a balm to the soul of the Jones family. As Keller says, they were being "driven like a nail deep into the love of God." Their Heavenly Father was close. They would never be the same.

"The Family Nest"

I had received a guitar for Christmas and wasted no time starting formal lessons. Amazingly, the three chords (D, G, and A7) and basic strumming patterns I learned the first week equipped me to play pretty much every song I knew. I was a natural and had an impressive repertoire of church choruses down before my fingertips had time to grow callouses. It wasn't long before I left classical instruction behind. Playing by ear (or at least "by heart") seemed so much more fun and efficient than learning how to read music!

This guitar had been an instrument of comfort to me in the early months of my musical endeavors, as Mom's illness confined her to bed. I spent many hours singing songs not only *about* God, but also *to* Him. His presence was tangible to me, in spite of the songs being simple and my skills unpolished. I remember going into my parent's bedroom on one occasion in particular and standing alongside the hospital bed where my Mom lay, her body weak and yellowed with jaundice. I softly strummed my guitar and sang the song I had practiced just for her:

> "Oh here comes Jesus, see Him walking on the water.
>
> He'll raise you up, and He'll help you to stand.

Oh here comes Jesus, He's the Master of the waves that roll.

Oh here comes Jesus, He'll save your soul."

We had been praying for Mom's healing and I fully expected she would be "raised up and standing" by the end of my song. None of us realized at the time that God would answer our prayers in a different way. She would receive her healing in heaven.

Early one spring morning Dad came into our bedrooms and shared with us kids that Mom had "gone home to be with the Lord." She had died in the night. As a 7-year-old, my ability to absorb and understand the implications of this sorrowful news was limited. Instead of tears, my first reaction was to ask whether or not we had to go to school that day, and relief that the answer was "no". The waves of grief, child-sized as they were, began to roll over me in the minutes and hours that followed. It was late that same morning, guitar in hand, I went searching for a private place to mourn. I have no idea why I ended up on the roof of the chicken coop in the back of our property. Perhaps I thought the higher elevation got me closer to heaven where Mom now resided. I don't know if anyone else had knowledge of my whereabouts, but God sure knew where I was. I know because He met me there and gave me a song:

"If you believe in the Lord Jesus Christ, you'll live eternally, forevermore.

You'll just be shoutin' hallelujah, praisin' the Lord,

can't you just picture you and me holdin' hands,

runnin' right through those open gates of glory?

We'll see His loving face, just filled with love and grace,

and Praise Him forevermore;

if you only believe, in the Lord Jesus Christ."

10: Father's Comfort – "The Family Nest"

I am still amazed at how personal and powerful God revealed Himself to be in those moments. He made heaven so real to me. I could see my Mom healed, happy, holding Jesus hand and "running right through the open gates of glory." My journey of grief did not end with that experience, but it proceeded from there in solid hope.

My sisters and I wanted to sleep with Dad during those early nights of grief. We all agreed that close to him was the only place to be. We accommodated that consensus by rearranging his room. It literally became a *bed*room as we got busy pushing several beds together, making one giant one. We were quite satisfied with our solution, until bedtime. It was then we realized the flaw in our plan; there were too many of us to all be able to sleep next to Dad at the same time. We worked that out diplomatically by deciding to take turns, rotating one spot over each night. As the old song goes, "...there were five in the bed and the little one said, roll over, roll over. So they all rolled over and one fell out, there were four in the bed and the little one said roll over." Our rolling over regularly took us close to the edge of the bed, but I'm happy to report that no one actually ever "fell out" and ended up on the floor.

I don't remember exactly how many nights we slept together in our giant nest. I wish I could recall the conversations we had, the prayers we prayed, the stories Dad told, the memories of Mom we shared together (inducing both giggling and tears) as we drifted off to sleep each night. Sadly, most of these particulars have faded from my memory.

What I mostly remember is a feeling of deep, healing, comfort. That snapshot memory of us at that time reminds me of Jesus, though rejected, telling his people, *"O Jerusalem...how often I have longed to gather your children together, as a hen gathers her chicks under her wings..."* (Matthew 23:37). I'm sure Dad didn't get much sleep those nights. Have you ever noticed how much room little kids take up in bed? Squished and crowded as we were, I'd still like to think our impromptu nest brought him some measure of comfort as well.

> *"Even though I walk through the darkest valley, I will fear no evil, for you are with me; your rod and your staff, they comfort me."* —Psalm 23:4

The five stages of grief are commonly described as: 1) Denial, 2) Anger, 3) Bargaining, 4) Depression and 5) Acceptance. While we all walk through grief uniquely, these stages simply define some of the common terrain experienced by people who have suffered loss. We don't experience these stages in a clean, lineal march. They are more like random waves in a choppy sea, tossing us about quite unexpectedly.

As Christians, we must allow ourselves to experience grief. It is not a lack of faith; it's a normal and healthy way to respond to loss. We must not rush our grieving process. It can take years for us to feel somewhat normal again. Truly dealing with grief is hard work. Though it may feel that this "night time" of our soul may last forever, God promises us that there will be a "morning" again. Psalm 30:5 tells us that, *"Weeping may stay for the night, but rejoicing comes in the morning."*

In their attempt to be helpful, well-meaning friends may say things to us in our grief that don't actually help, or may even be hurtful. Their intentions may be good, but comments like, "It must have been her time to go", or "God must have wanted another angel in heaven", or even, "Just try to be strong for the children" have no value in helping us through our pain. There is no getting around it - grief is messy business. We are emotionally raw and desperate. The best support our friends can offer is to be graciously present, patient, and to provide practical help.

Many of the Psalms were written in times of grief, loss, and anguish. Our pastoral advice to grieving people over the years has been to spend time in the Psalms. In these ancient, inspired songs we see both the soaring heights of praise and the ragged edge of sorrow. They can help us be real with our pain before God. He is not offended if yell at Him. He can take it, and the exercise will likely do us some good! David, primary writer of these

Psalms, knew a life of ups and downs, triumphs and tragedies. God saw to it that his words were recorded in the Bible as holy literature for both Jews and Christians. Perhaps one of the greatest gifts of the Psalms is helping us work through our own grief.

Each of us will at some point have our own experience with deep grief in this life. We may try to share the story with words, but words can never describe the true depths of anguish in our soul. These are places only "the God of all comfort" can tread with us. When we feel nothing else, we feel His breath on our cheek. When our hearts are like stone, it is His hand we feel on our shoulder. The words of the Scottish minister and author, Alexander MacLaren, capture so beautifully how Jesus travels with us through our grief.

> *"Oh, when we are journeying through the murky night and the dark woods of affliction and sorrow, it is something to find here and there a spray broken, or a leafy stem bent down with the tread of His foot and the brush of His hand as He passed; and to remember that the path He trod He has hallowed, and thus to find lingering fragrance and hidden strength in the remembrance of Him as "in all points tempted like as we are," bearing grief for us, bearing grief with us, bearing grief like us."* —Alexander MacLaren (1826-1910)

There are times to be alone with God in grief. At other times we must "push the beds together" with our loved ones. They provide the real touch of the Father for us in our loss. There need not be words...just presence. And with that presence we feel the comfort of our Heavenly Father.

Journey to the Father

Get into the Story:

1. What was the deepest grief you ever experienced? How did you deal with it?

2. What relationships were most meaningful to you when you had to "push the beds together" for comfort?

3. One of the titles of the Holy Spirit is "the Comforter." How was His ministry seen through your time of deep sorrow?

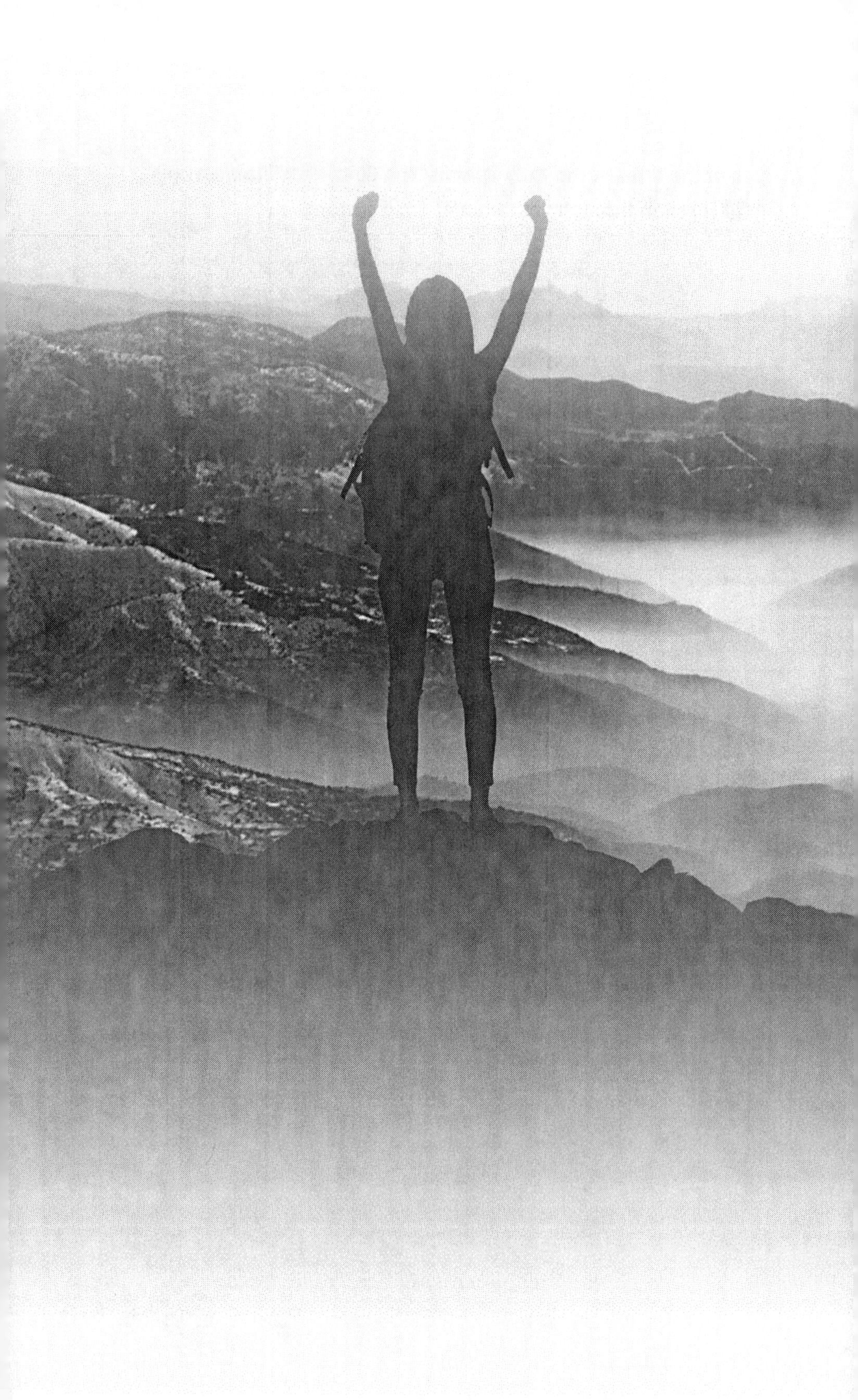

11

Father's Praise

> "Because thy lovingkindness is better than life, my lips shall praise thee." —Psalm 63:3 (KJV)

Our heavenly Father is deserving of praise, and yet, that is not our natural response when things don't go our way. How do we act when we're disappointed with people, God, or ourselves? What do we do when we feel powerless? How do we handle deep grief? The answers to these questions are many and varied, but "worship" is not likely among them. While worship is a very unnatural place to start, it is a supernaturally possible place to end.

"There is no attempt in Scripture to whitewash the anguish of God's people when they undergo suffering. They argue with God, they complain to God, they weep before God. Theirs is not a faith that leads to dry-eyed stoicism, but to a faith so robust it wrestles with God." - D.A. Carson

Notice that King David, a man after God's own heart, begins many of his songs crying out against God for His perceived absence, bemoaning his problem, and cursing his enemies. He says such raw things as: *"Why, Lord, do you stand far off? Why do you hide yourself in times of trouble"* (Psalm 10:1)? *"I am overwhelmed with troubles and my life draws near to death. I am counted among those who go down to the pit; I am like one without strength"* (Psalm 88:3-4) and about his enemies he says, *"Break the teeth in their mouths, O God"* (Psalm 58:6). But, as David pours out his heart to the Lord, we see a lifting of his perspective. There is an internal transformation that takes place as he grieves in God's presence. What often began as pessimism from David ended in praise! For example Psalm 69 begins with, *"Save me, O God, for the waters have come up to my neck. I sink in the miry depths, where there is no foothold. I have come into the deep waters; the floods engulf me. I am worn out calling for help; my throat is parched. My eyes fail, looking for my God"* (v. 1-3) and ends with, *"I will praise God's name in song and glorify him with thanksgiving... The poor will see and be glad—you who seek God, may your hearts live! The Lord hears the needy and does not despise his captive people"* (v. 30-33).

What was the transcendent reality between David's pain and his praise? How did his faith always come out on top with a heavenly perspective? The answer is found in the burning rubble of Ziklag. We read this remarkable story in I Samuel 30. Before becoming king of Israel, David was hiding out among the Philistines. He and his army of skilled warriors would go out on secret missions against the enemies of Israel. On one occasion, when David and all his men were out on a raid, the Amalekites sacked Ziklag and hauled off all the women and children of David's army. When David and his men returned and saw their families had been taken captive, they wept until they had no more strength to weep. The anguish of David's men was so severe they spoke of killing him! Verse 6 tells of David's response: *"David was greatly distressed because the men were talking of stoning him; each one was bitter in spirit because of his sons and daughters. But David found strength in the Lord his God."* The KJV translates this phrase: *"but David encouraged himself in the LORD his God."*

When everyone else's faith was sinking in despair, David's faith rose up as he encouraged himself in the Lord. He may have gotten away in a private place with his harp, allowing the melodies of his shepherding days to wash over his spirit as he sat down and began to strum. Perhaps he recalled the past faithfulness of God in his deliverance from the lion, bear, Goliath, and even jealous King Saul. He likely pondered the attributes of his Father God: faithful, almighty, protecting, defending, faultless, and holy. While the other men in David's army were awash with grief, David was building himself up with what he knew to be true of God. He called this *"magnifying the Lord"* in a Psalm he wrote just two years earlier. The lyrics would have bolstered his faith now:

> *"I will bless the Lord at all times;*
> his *praise shall continually be in my mouth.*
> *My soul makes its boast in the Lord;*
> let *the humble hear and be glad.*
> *Oh, magnify the Lord with me,*
> and *let us exalt his name together!"* —Psalm 34:1-3

Pastor Brian Zahnd addresses this beautifully when he writes: "Magnify means 'to enlarge or make bigger in perspective.' When we magnify a small object with a magnifying glass, a microscope or a telescope, we don't change its reality. We don't make the object we are observing any bigger; we change our perception of it. We cannot make God any bigger than He already is—you can't increase omnipotence—but you can magnify, or diminish, *your perspective* of God. Perspective has everything to do with whether you are encouraged or discouraged."

Pastor Denver Jones and his five children were in the throes of grief in the spring of 1972 following Dorothy's lost battle with breast cancer. Denver's world had fallen apart, and I'm sure he wasn't the only one wondering how in the world he was going to put it back together. Though many people graciously offered support, he seemed helplessly held captive by the strong grip of grief. While pity beckoned, God called his faith to something higher - the healing path of praise.

"Mourning into Dancing"

It was a common occurrence for Dad to break out in spontaneous praise. This wasn't a trite and shallow, "yeah rah rah" denial-of-reality way of life for him. His random shouts of "glory," may have made it sound as though he lived on a spiritual mountaintop, but we knew they were forged in the valley. The way he generally wore the joy of the Lord on his sleeve made his love for God contagious. For Dad, worship was a normal reflex to life's happenings, good or bad. He used to say some things in life are better "caught" than "taught." This was certainly true for me in how I came to understand what it means to live a life of authentic worship.

Dad cared for us kids after Mom died to the point of making malt-o-meal for three of us to our own individual liking. Pat liked hers lumpy, Mary's preferred consistency was runny, and I needed mine just thick enough to "make roads in it". His daily displays of care and affection went a long way in moving us through our grief. As for Dad, it would take more than custom-made breakfast cereal to heal his broken heart. Dad and mom shared true oneness throughout their fourteen years of marriage. Losing her left him feeling lost.

A kind friend made a small country cabin available to Dad early in his journey of grief, should he feel the need to get away. He did make his way there eventually. Not sure what else to do, he decided to take a walk. The calendar said it was spring, but the sound of silence revealed that the birds had not yet been informed of this news. The icy winds, frozen lake and barren landscape seemed a fitting reflection of what he felt inside...cold, dead. Finding no comfort in nature's lifeless display, he returned to his cabin of refuge.

Dad had a history with God. Though very alone, he had an intimate relationship with the God of all comfort. He thought that now, more than any other time, would be a good time for Him to speak. Out of the dark quiet came His clear words to Dad's heart: "Give thanks." "Oh Lord," Dad responded with weak and weary faith. "I don't have the strength. Right now I need you to minister to me." The Comforter's words continued with gentle persistence. "Give thanks. Give thanks."

Dad's response began with reluctance. "I love you, Lord," he finally managed to voice. Words he knew to be true, although they were void of any feeling at the time. "Lord, You are worthy of my worship," he continued as a sheer act of obedience. "Lord, You are good...You are faithful...You do all things well." Eventually, the tenuous trickle of praise became transforming torrents of worship. Tears flowed, singing, dancing and shouts of joy ensued. Like David, God had turned his mourning into dancing! (Psalm 30:11).

Deliverance came not in the denial of his pain, but in the declaration of a greater reality; the grace of God! His circumstances remained the same, but his perspective was forever changed. He had many more miles of grief to traverse, but he could press on in the light of hope instead of under the dark, oppressive cloud of despair. He carried on as his Heavenly Father carried him. He cared for us out of the comfort he received from Christ.

As children, we gave little thought to *how* dad was able to care for us the way he did. All we knew was he made awesome malt-o-meal. His supernatural revelation was fleshed out in practical application. His faith was substantive, not superficial. His winsome holiness was both endearing and enduring.

He pointed us to the solidness of Christ so many years ago when everything in our world was shaking. It remains our firm foundation to this day.

Like all of us, Denver faced both joy and sorrow... times to weep and times to laugh, times to mourn and times to dance (Ecclesiastes 3:4). The thing that so greatly impacted his children was that he responded *to both* with worship. We can also think of David, who with great joy, worshiped with all his might, in celebration of the Ark of the Covenant returning to Jerusalem (2 Samuel 6:14-15). Also Paul and Silas, who prayed and sang hymns to God...at midnight... in prison. In response, God caused an earthquake to shake the foundations of the prison, bringing deliverance to all who were in chains (Acts 16:16-26).

Sometimes our worship comes with rejoicing, *"Sing joyfully to the Lord, you righteous"* (Psalm 33:1) and sometimes it comes with agony, *"Out of the depths I cry to you, O Lord"* (Psalm 130:1). Both are fitting for the people of God. Psalm 33:1 says, *"Sing joyfully to the Lord, you righteous; it is fitting for the upright to praise him."*

Perhaps the greatest example of the power of praise is seen in II Chronicles 20 when a vast army of three kingdoms formed an alliance to wipe out the people of Judah. King Jehoshaphat knew that his own army was no match against the sea of warriors coming against him. He turned to God for help and proclaimed a time of prayer and fasting for the whole nation. While gathered in the temple, a young priest prophesied by the Spirit to those gathered, *"You will not need to fight in this battle. Position yourselves, stand still, and see the salvation of the Lord, who is with you! Do not be afraid or discouraged because of this vast army. For the battle is not yours, but God's"* (II Chronicles 20:15).

The next day, as the army of God's people were preparing for battle, King Jehoshaphat *"appointed men to sing to the Lord and to praise him for the splendor of his holiness as they went out at the head of the army, saying: 'Give thanks to the Lord, for his love endures forever.' As they began to sing and praise, the Lord set ambushes against the men of Ammon and Moab and Mount Seir who were invading Judah, and they were defeated"* (v. 21-22). It took the men of Judah three whole days to haul home the plunder from the destroyed army!

When facing a crisis, our enemy, the Devil, would have us magnify our problem. God's solution is not to minimize our problems, but to magnify the Lord! Notice what the singers sang as they led the army that day, *'Give thanks to the Lord, for his love endures forever.'* What if this powerful phrase was on our lips the next time we faced a crisis? In the case of Jehoshaphat, the Lord fought for him. All he had to do was to praise!

Get into the Story:

1. When you are hurting, are you able to be honest with God and others about the depth of your pain?

11: Father's Praise – *"Mourning into Dancing"*

2. Have you ever sincerely praised God in the midst of your pain? How did God show Himself strong for you?

3. Psalm 23 says, *"He restores my soul."* Describe a time when you truly sensed the Lord graciously restoring your inner being.

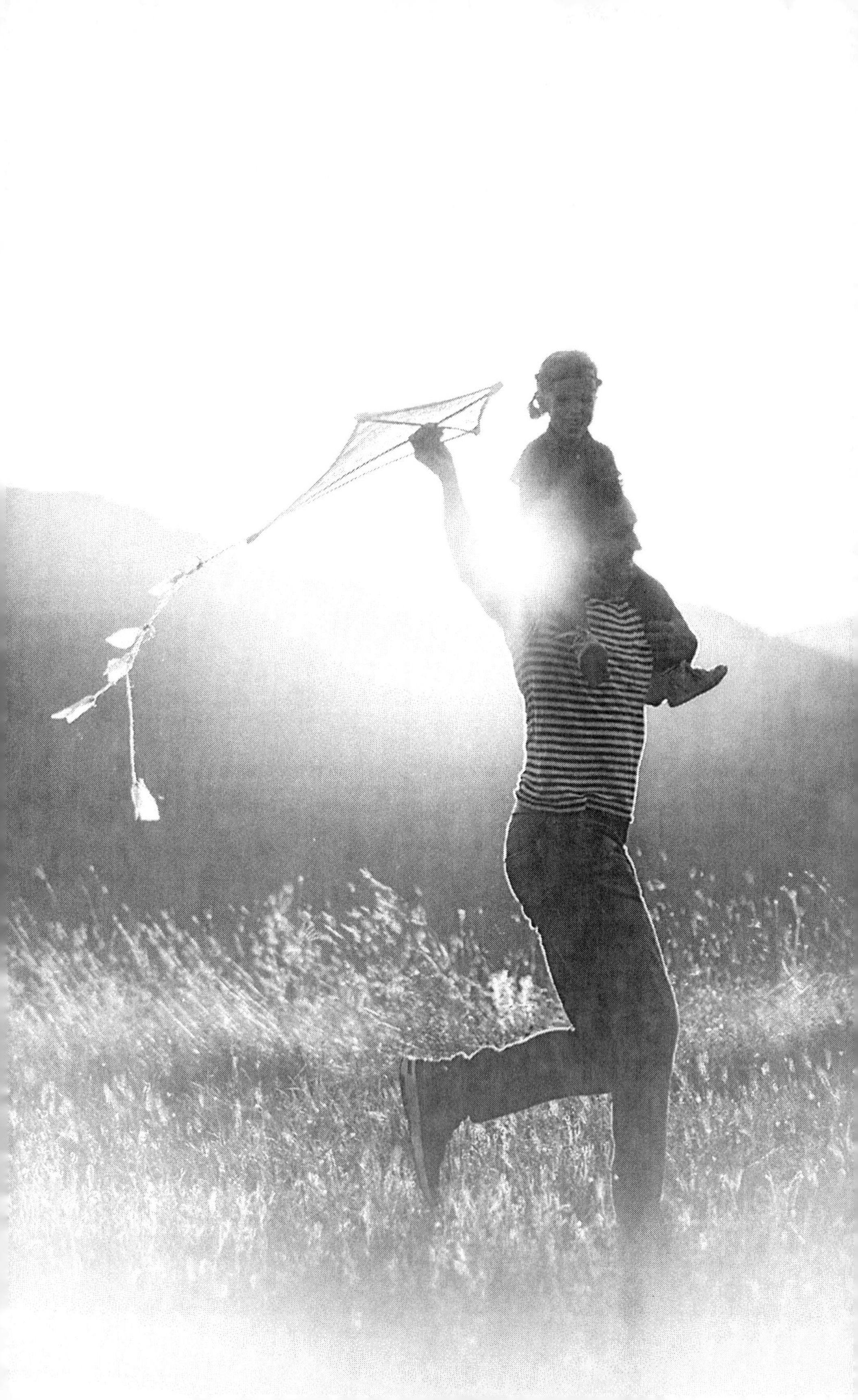

12

Father's Grace

> *"I am content to fill a little space if God be glorified."* —Susanna Wesley

Our Father cherishes us, not because of what we do for Him, but for who we are - His dearly beloved children. It is because of Christ Jesus that we are brought into God's favor. None of this is based on our own human merit, but on God's grace. All of our serving, be it large or small, leaves a trail of blessing when it springs from our awareness of God's great pleasure in us. If we get this wrong, we can fall into the subtle trap of trying to win our Father's favor based on our performance and good works.

The Apostle Paul underscored this fact when he wrote, *"For by grace you are saved through faith, and this is not from yourselves, it is the gift of God; it is not from works, so that no one can boast. For we are his workmanship, having been created in Christ Jesus for good works that God prepared beforehand so we may do them"* (Ephesians 2:8-10). This passage makes it clear that, while good works do not save us, there are works that God has prepared in advance for us to do. Being saved by grace does not put us on a track of inactivity; rather, it launches us into a life of divine purpose and invites us to ask at every turn, "What would you have me to do, Father?"

> "To say that God has prepared the good works in advance in his sovereign purpose is also to stress in the strongest possible way that believers' good deeds cannot be chalked up to their own resolve, but are due solely to divine grace." —Andrew T. Lincoln

We may get stuck in thinking that if we cannot do a "big" thing for our Father, we don't have anything of value to offer. We reason little things are inconsequential and unexceptional. So, we end up doing nothing...not even a "small work." We forget that the Father's standard of measurement is different than ours. In God's Kingdom economy, little morsels become full banquets; a small word of encouragement becomes a discourse of hope. I wonder how many times we fail to see or simply walk right past the *"good works that God prepares"* because they seem too menial and insignificant. Mother Teresa said, "We can do no great things – only small things with great love."

Denver Jones was a church-planting pastor for many years and did many "small works" with joy and without fanfare. What he sowed in secret, he reaped openly. Still, there were times when he wavered and wondered if he was doing any good for Christ. I remember him telling me on more than one occasion, "Sonny, many a ministry has been saved by the smallest word of encouragement." Not only was he equipping me with a great truth, he was speaking from his own experience. Each simple gift he was given whether a kind word; a listening ear; a testimony of how he had been used by God; or even a folded up twenty dollar bill, became a means of grace to his life. Even when our "small works" go unnoticed on earth, our Heavenly Father sees them. We will only realize their full value when we hear Him say, *"Well done, good and faithful servant, you have been faithful in the little things..."* (Matthew 25:23).

"Father's Day Foibles"

It was Father's Day, 1972. Two months had passed since mom's death, and we were thankful for an occasion that would shift our focus to something of a celebratory nature. My two older sisters and I asked Dad what we could get him for Father's Day, not because we had hope of him offering any helpful clues as to what he really wanted, but because we never tired of hearing him ask (in jest) for the gift of his dreams – a brand new snowmobile. Imagining our dignified, British, white-shirt-and-tie-wearing dad tearing around on such a machine always made us laugh. That bit of comic relief behind us, my sisters and I scrounged up several fists full of change and headed to the nearest drugstore to purchase a gift more within our means. A new red clip-on tie perhaps? (He always wore clip-on ties, and red was his favorite color.) A new pen set? (We were always losing his pens.) A new china teacup? (Like every good Welshman, Dad enjoyed a good cup of tea and held fast to the conviction that it tasted best when sipped from a china teacup.) However, with less than two dollars to spend, the best we could come up with was a fingernail clipper. We did have a little money left over, which we included in the gift along with a note suggesting he consider saving up for some shorts. Poor dad didn't own one pair of shorts. We didn't realize at the time that shorts don't go very well with a white shirt and tie.

The cards were prepared, the gift was wrapped, and we piled onto his bed that morning for the big Father's Day presentation. Dad read and made over each simple hand-made card as if we were all acclaimed poets and artists. This was going better than expected. Now it was time for the present. My sisters and I exchanged nervous glances as Dad carefully unwrapped the package.

All of a sudden we were feeling sheepish about our meager gift. Anticipation built as he reached inside the little unwrapped box, fishing around a while before revealing his catch. The moment we saw the nail clipper dangling by its chain from his fingers, all of us spontaneously erupted into tears. To us it was like a fish he needed to throw back into the water, too small to keep. Our hope was extravagance. Our reality was embarrassment. He deserved so much more! Between sobs, we made our best attempt at an apology, trying to explain how we would have gotten him a snowmobile if we could have only afforded it.

At that point, he turned his attention from his emotionally distraught daughters to his new fingernail clipper. He examined it closely and began noting how especially well-crafted it was and how much more useful it was than a snowmobile would ever be, and what a relief it was that he would never have to buy gasoline in order to use it.

Then he saw the loose change and read the accompanying note. He said that he couldn't think of any better addition to his wardrobe than a pair of shorts and couldn't figure out how he had gotten by this long without them. His delight in us was sincere, but his elaborate and exaggerated assessment of our simple gifts became so funny that we started laughing at the ridiculousness of the whole situation. We laughed until we were once again in tears, except this time they were tears of joy.

How could there be any other response when you had believed yourself to be a disappointment to your dad, only to find instead you were his delight.

> "Nobody made a greater mistake than he who did nothing because he could only do a little." — Edmund Burke

Our Heavenly Father is worthy of so much more than we could ever give Him. After all, what of any significance can we give to the "Guy who has everything"? Our standing with the Father is not based on what we bring to the table but what Jesus brought to the cross. It's not the size of our gifts, but the source that matters. We exert time and energy scrounging up fists full of change when God has already freely and abundantly supplied all we need in order to please Him. Anything of value we bring *to* Him comes *from* Him. We love Him because He first loved us. If we get this turned around, we end up feeling deficient and our Father ends up with a pair of shorts He didn't need in the first place! No gift is too small that flows from our Father's love. This is what the Jones girls learned from their dad on Father's Day.

Throughout our own children's grade school and high school years, we made a practice of laying our hands on them and blessing them before they left for the day. We told them, "You are blessed to be a blessing" and then, off to school they'd go. That daily commission cemented something in all four of them that they have carried into their adult lives. They learned that they are both receivers and dispensers of God's graces. Jesus told His disciples, *"Freely you have received; freely give"* (Matthew 10:8). As Christians, we have the treasures of the Kingdom of God living within us. Although we may feel under resourced and ill equipped in the natural, we must know this truer reality: we have received the Father's blessing and always have something of the life of God to give. The source of this life-giving grace does not originate with us but flows freely to us from our loving Heavenly Father. We are blessed to be a blessing.

One of Jesus' most amazing miracles was the feeding of the five thousand. While this story is recorded in all four gospels, John gives us an insight that the other gospels do not. John identifies the source of the five loaves and two fish which were about to become a miracle meal. Read this familiar story with fresh eyes:

> *When Jesus looked up and saw a great crowd coming toward him, he said to Philip, "Where shall we buy bread for these people to eat?" He asked this only to test him, for he already had in mind what he was going to do. Philip answered him, "It would take more than half a year's wages to buy enough bread for each one to have a bite!" Another of*

12: Father's Grace – "Father's Day Foibles"

his disciples, Andrew, Simon Peter's brother, spoke up, "Here is a boy with five small barley loaves and two small fish, but how far will they go among so many?"

Jesus said, "Have the people sit down." There was plenty of grass in that place, and they sat down (about five thousand men were there). Jesus then took the loaves, gave thanks, and distributed to those who were seated as much as they wanted. He did the same with the fish.

When they had all had enough to eat, he said to his disciples, "Gather the pieces that are left over. Let nothing be wasted." So they gathered them and filled twelve baskets with the pieces of the five barley loaves left over by those who had eaten.

—John 6:5-13

"Here is a boy" is all that we learn of this willing young lad. I wonder if Andrew, Jesus' disciple, passed him by several times before approaching him thinking that what he had was much too scant to be of any help. His lunch consisted of just five barley loaves and two fish, and the gospel account is careful to identify both the loaves and the fish as "small." In those days, barley was the grain of the poor. It was cheap to grow, easy to buy, and usually used for horse feed. The fish were likely sardines, a common catch of net fishermen on the Sea of Galilee. When smoked or dried, it became an ideal travel food for the people of the region. We learn very little about the boy in this story. Were his parents with him? Why was he in the crowd that day? Did he know someone who had been healed by Jesus and want to meet Him personally? The boy is never named, and we don't see him appear anywhere else in Scripture. All we know is that he was present and willingly gave his lunch away to Jesus.

The Apostle Andrew commented about the smallness of the boy's contribution of bread and fish by saying, *"How far will they go among so many?"* Again we are struck with the natural insufficiency of this boy's gift. But what did our Lord do? He gladly received it, gave thanks, and distributed it. The result was a well-fed crowd and twelve baskets of food left over! Too many times, we look at our contribution and think that what we have is too small and insignificant. We wonder, "Who am I to even participate in what Jesus is doing?" What if the boy in this story had that kind of attitude? He and everyone else in the crowd would have missed out on an amazing miracle and on lunch as well. Like this young boy, our focus must not be on our inadequacy but on Christ's sufficiency. In His hands, our meager gift becomes His miraculous supply. Whatever we bring to God in our poverty, He multiplies for great provision. Nothing is wasted that is entrusted to Him. Multiplying the small, weak and foolish things is one of the confounding laws of how our Father advances His kingdom. *"But God chose the foolish things of the world to shame the wise; God chose the weak things of the world to shame the strong"* (I Corinthians 1:27).

The gift of a nail clipper and loose change from the Jones girls was meager for sure, but Denver received it with joy. His delight was in them, not the size of their gift. Their love for him was more than enough. This is much like the Gospel story where Jesus praises the widow who, out of poverty, gave her last two copper coins. Her simple gift displayed extravagant love. In Mark 12:41-44 Jesus said, *"I tell you the truth, this poor widow has put more into the offering box than all the others."* Our Father takes great joy in our simplest gifts when sincerely given.

Get into the Story:

1. Have you ever felt embarrassed by giving a gift you thought to be too small to someone you love? What did you learn from that experience?

_____

_____

_____

12: Father's Grace – *"Father's Day Foibles"*

2. What are some of the "small works" you have contributed only to see God use them in a big way?

3. Do you believe that "you are blessed to be a blessing?" If so, how can you begin to give out of the deposit Christ has made in you?

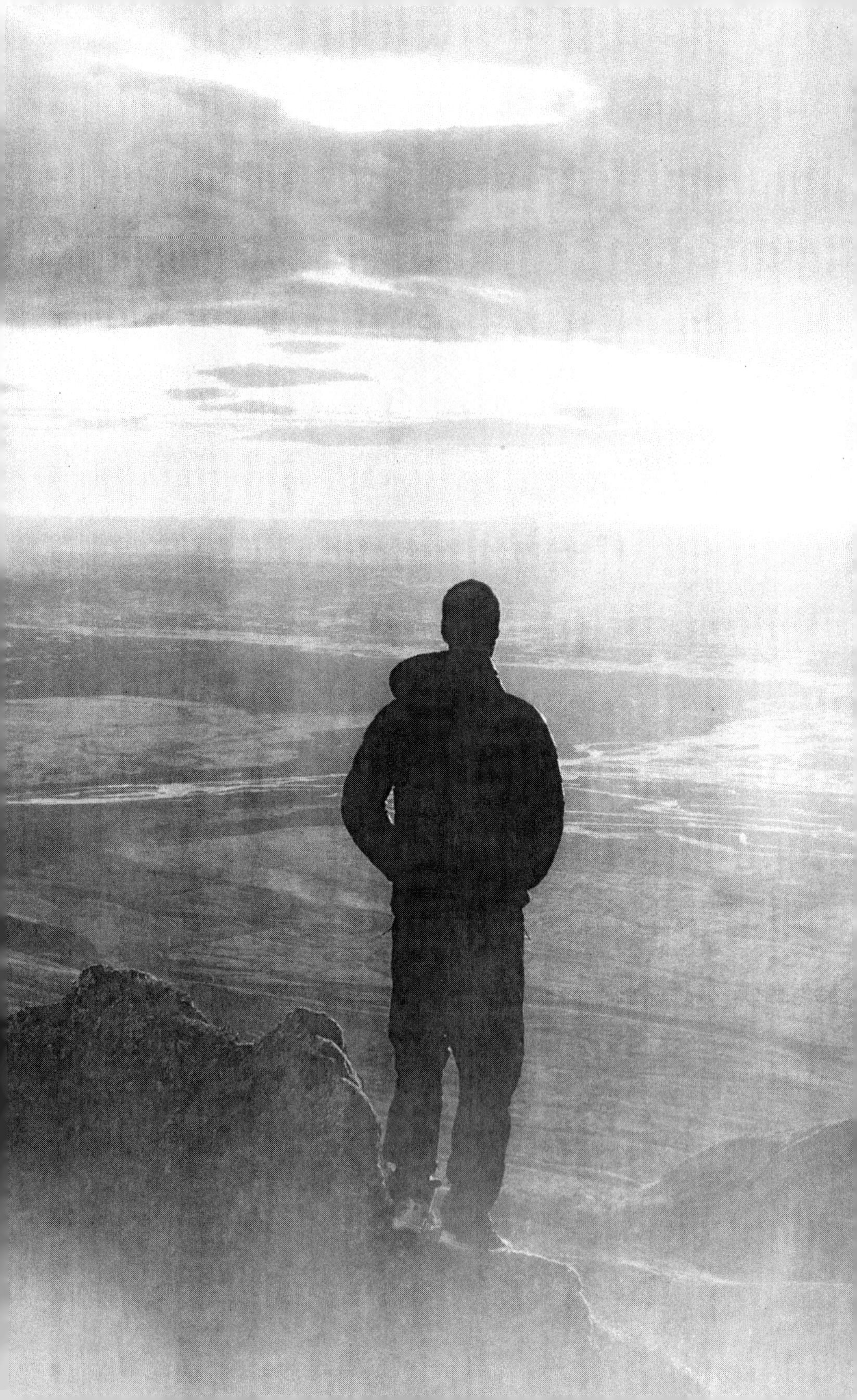

13

Father's Will

> *Jesus replied, "You don't understand now what I am doing, but someday you will." —John 13:7 (NLT)*

What is it about human nature that we don't like being told, "no?" Why is it that our desires always demand to be answered with a "yes"? The answer can be traced all the way back to the Garden of Eden.

God had placed Adam and Eve in the midst of His perfect and glorious creation where everything was "yes", with the exception of only one "no". They bought the lie of Satan that God was holding out on them and demanded a yes to God's one no. Consequently, they got themselves (and us) into a heap of trouble!

Journey to the Father

When we pray, we can be assured that God hears us and that He always answers every prayer. He may answer with a "yes", "no", "not yet", or "yes, but this is the way I want to do it". Sometimes we approach the Lord much like James and John did in Mark 10:3: *"we want you to do for us whatever we ask."* We may not be so bold as to use those exact words, but this is our attitude: "Jesus, we want a blank check. We want You to leverage all Your omnipotence and pull this off for us in the manner we've prescribed. Thank you very much!"

James 1:17 tells us our Father is *"the Giver of good gifts."* From II Corinthians 1:20 we read that *"every promise God has made is "yes" in Christ Jesus."* Jesus also tells us *"whatever we ask for in His name, He will do"* John 14:13. We also know that if we ask anything *"according to his will, He hears us and that we have what we asked of him"* 1 John 5:14-15. With all these promises in God's word, why aren't all of our requests granted? There is a clue in the last passage above: we must ask *according to His will*. Our requests must find themselves within the sovereign will of our wise and loving Father.

When we really want a "yes" from God, it's hard to be open to any other answer. We can get solely fixated on the positive outcome of our desire and approach our Father like a heavenly gumball machine – just put in the quarter (prayer), turn the knob (faith) and out comes our big, delicious gumball (the exact thing we are asking for). Yet, this is *not* the way prayer works.

If God has ever told you "no," you're in good company. King David asked God if he could build Him a temple...God said "no" (1 Chronicles 28). The Apostle Paul begged God three times to remove a trial that was like a thorn in his flesh...God said "no" (2 Corinthians 12:7-10). Jesus prayed in the Garden of Gethsemane for God to remove the bitter cup of suffering from Him... God said "no" (Mark 14:32-42). The apostle Paul and his companions were on their second missionary journey and praying about ministering to the north and south. The Spirit prohibited them...God said "no" (Acts 16:6-10). These divine deterrents were not a rebuke from their Father, but a gracious invitation to something much superior.

13: Father's Will – "Monkey See, Monkey Want"

> *"And we know that in all things God works for the good of those who love him, who have been called according to his purpose."*
> —Romans 8:28

I (Sonny) remember intently asking God if I could date a girl to whom I was particularly attracted. Even though I was a young man, I was spiritually mature enough to realize that I should seek God's will in the matter. What I didn't realize is that my heart was only willing to hear a "yes" from the Lord. As the days and weeks wore on, I became increasingly frustrated that I was not hearing anything from Him. "Come on, God, I am earnestly seeking your direction about this girl, the least you could do is speak to me!" Still there was silence. The breakthrough finally came after the Holy Spirit showed me that I had to lay all the cards on the table. He spoke clearly to my heart, "Sonny, I will not reveal My will to you until you come to a point of being willing to hear *any* answer I give you."

With the grace of this revelation came the grace to surrender this decision to Him. When He said "no", there was enough work done in my heart that I was able to accept His perfect will. When I met "Ms. Right," I could see that behind His initial "no", was God's better "yes". Now, after 30 years of marriage to Becky, I'm still saying, "Amen!" My big lesson through that experience was this: if I am to receive heaven's direction, I must first yield my personal ambition.

> *"Prayer is not a convenient device for imposing our will on God, or for bending his will to ours, but the prescribed way of subordinating our will to his. It is by prayer that we seek God's will, embrace it and align ourselves with it. Every true prayer is a variation on the theme 'your will be done.'"*
> —John R. W. Stott

"Monkey See, Monkey Want"

Did you ever desire something so intensely that you were convinced of two things: with it you would be forever satisfied and without it you just couldn't go on living? My sister Pat and I felt this way about our want, no our *need,* for a pair of monkeys; one each to call our own. We pictured something chimpanzee-like that could be taught to do entertaining tricks and trained to clean the bedroom we shared. If they were useful to NASA for flights into space, and to scientists for important studies, surely they would be helpful to an ordinary family around the house. Our imaginations went wild with possibilities. We could dress them up and take them to school. They would sit on our laps at church, clapping their hands along with the rest of us during singing time. We could teach them math problems and they could teach us how to swing from tree to tree. Our vision was clear, our resolve firm, we *had* to have our monkeys.

Dad was a widower at this time which put him at a great disadvantage in this particular situation. He and Mom had loved all us kids equally and unquestionably, yet we learned there were benefits to asking one of them over another in certain instances when help or permission was being sought. Which one to ask, depended on the nature of the situation. Generally speaking, if we truly needed something, we went to mom. If we were trying to get away with something, we went to Dad. My parents had walked in a high level of unity and agreement, so trying to play one against the other usually backfired, but there were times when a well-placed plea posed to the right parent upped the odds of a "yes". Mom loved saying "yes" if our requests were reasonable and within her ability to grant them. Dad loved saying "yes" while sometimes being *unaware* of practicalities. He was a bit more "free flowing" and tended to ask fewer questions. Had both parents been in the picture at the time, Dad would definitely have been the one with whom to open the monkey discussion.

13: Father's Will – *"Monkey See, Monkey Want"*

Pat and I became consumed with the passion to be monkey owners about a year after mom had died. Perhaps it was a diversion from our grief. Poor Dad. It was two against one and his defenses were at an all time low when we launched our monkey campaign. Bypassing subtlety altogether, we went straight into begging, loud and long, and then longer and louder. In our estimation, a "yes" would be simple and to his great advantage. We promised he would never have to buy us anything else, and that we would never again be bored ("bored" was a nasty word as far as Dad was concerned). Further, we vowed to bear the responsibility for all monkey chores. After all, how hard could it be? (We pictured them potty trained, well-mannered, self-grooming and able to peel their own bananas.)

Dad genuinely wanted to satisfy our desire. The day we convinced him to take us to a pet store that had a monkey, we were sure he was honestly considering the possibility. Seeing as this store had a sole monkey, we thought we might even be happy sharing one between us. Disappointingly, this pet store monkey was nothing like a chimpanzee. It was small, spidery, and barred its teeth when you went near it. Only momentarily disenchanted, we convinced ourselves that this one would just require a little extra training. In no time it would be with us in church, clapping *and* raising its hands along with us in worship. To our disappointment (but truly by a great mercy), it turned out the monkey was not for sale.

Though Dad sometimes had a tendency to overlook practical details, he was not foolish. He knew that though monkeys were what we wanted in the worst way, they were the last thing we really needed. It would have been disastrous, not to mention nearly impossible to acquire such a pet. He put up with more begging in this instance than I can imagine tolerating as a parent, but I think he wanted to give us the fun of dreaming for a while. Dad may have been slow with his "no", but the time came when the discussion was over for good.

The sense of utter need that Pat and I had for monkeys so many years ago seems absurd to me now. It illustrates how limited is the perspective of a child. Such is the case with us as children of God. We petition Him with desires, sincerely believing them to be what we truly want or need, but we don't always get what we ask for, at least not in the way or timeframe we expect. Our Heavenly Father, perfect in love and perspective, listens to us attentively and knows us fully. He answers our prayers according to what is truly best for us and most glorifying to Him. Even though Dad denied Pat and my request all those years ago, we never doubted his love for us. How much more has our Heavenly Father proved His love for us.

In case you are wondering, Pat and I were not permanently scarred by Dad's decision. We eventually got over our disappointment, moved on and settled for a mail order packet of Sea Monkeys!

Though Dad denied Pat and my request all those years ago, we never doubted his love for us. How much more has our Heavenly Father proved His love for us.

13: Father's Will – "Monkey See, Monkey Want"

> *"If the request is wrong, God says, No. If the timing is wrong, God says, Slow. If you are wrong, God says, Grow. But if the request is right, the timing is right and you are right, God says, Go!"* —Bill Hybels

Every time we approach our Father with a request, it is an exercise of faith. However, when we come fully submitting our will to His, that requires greater faith still. The greatest faith is not displayed as vividly in us when God is answering all our prayers as when His activity in and around us is less obvious. Our faith muscle is strengthened as we prayerfully wait, trusting Him to work out His purpose that lies beyond what we can see or understand. It is appropriate to boldly present our requests to God, but it is vitally important we entrust the outcomes to Him. The prayerful phrase, "Not my will, but Yours be done" is not a copout, nor is it a spiritual cliché. Rather, it is a sign of humility and ultimate surrender to the loving providence of God. Praying that God's will take preeminence over our request is powerful and biblical: Jesus prayed it (Luke 22:42), Peter submitted to it (Acts 11:167), the Apostle Paul was led by it (Acts 18:21), John was confident of it (I John 5:14) and James instructed us to make our plans according to it (James 3:15). Indeed, our prayers are purest when our will is fully submitted to Him.

B.M. Palmer in his book *Theology of Prayer*, tells of a woman who had been away from her children for many months and eagerly sought to secure a ticket to sail from New York harbor back to England. The longing she already felt in her heart for her children was intensified when she learned that the ship on which she intended to sail was already full. In her desperation, she cried out to God, only to find that all the other departing ships were also at capacity. Her journey home was delayed and she was required to wait in New York for an additional two weeks. However, her frustration was transformed to trust when she learned within days that the vessel that turned her away had sunk and was lying on the bottom of the Atlantic Ocean. Tragically and inexplicably, many good people perished on that ship that day.

This dear woman resented God's "no" until she saw the wider picture of his providential care for her.

When our desperate hearts "must have the monkey", it would be wise to remember that our Father has our best in mind. When we only want a "yes" from the Lord, it is important to remember the promise of Jeremiah 29:11, *"'For I know the plans I have for you,' declares the Lord, 'plans to prosper you and not to harm you, plans to give you hope and a future.'"* He is not out to frustrate our lives, but to fulfill them. This will help us reorient our heart and give Him preeminence in our desires. Psalm 37:4 says *"Take delight in the Lord, and he will give you the desires of your heart."* So, when we have to leave the store without the chimpanzee in our arms, remember that God may have just delivered us from a real monkey on our back!

Get into the Story:

1. Are you willing to sincerely use the phrase, *"not my will, but Yours be done"* when praying?

_____
_____
_____
_____
_____
_____
_____
_____

13: Father's Will – *"Monkey See, Monkey Want"*

2. How have you done historically with submitting your will to God when He said "no" to your desperate plea?

3. Think about and thank God for a time when your Father's "no" delivered you from a real monkey on your back.

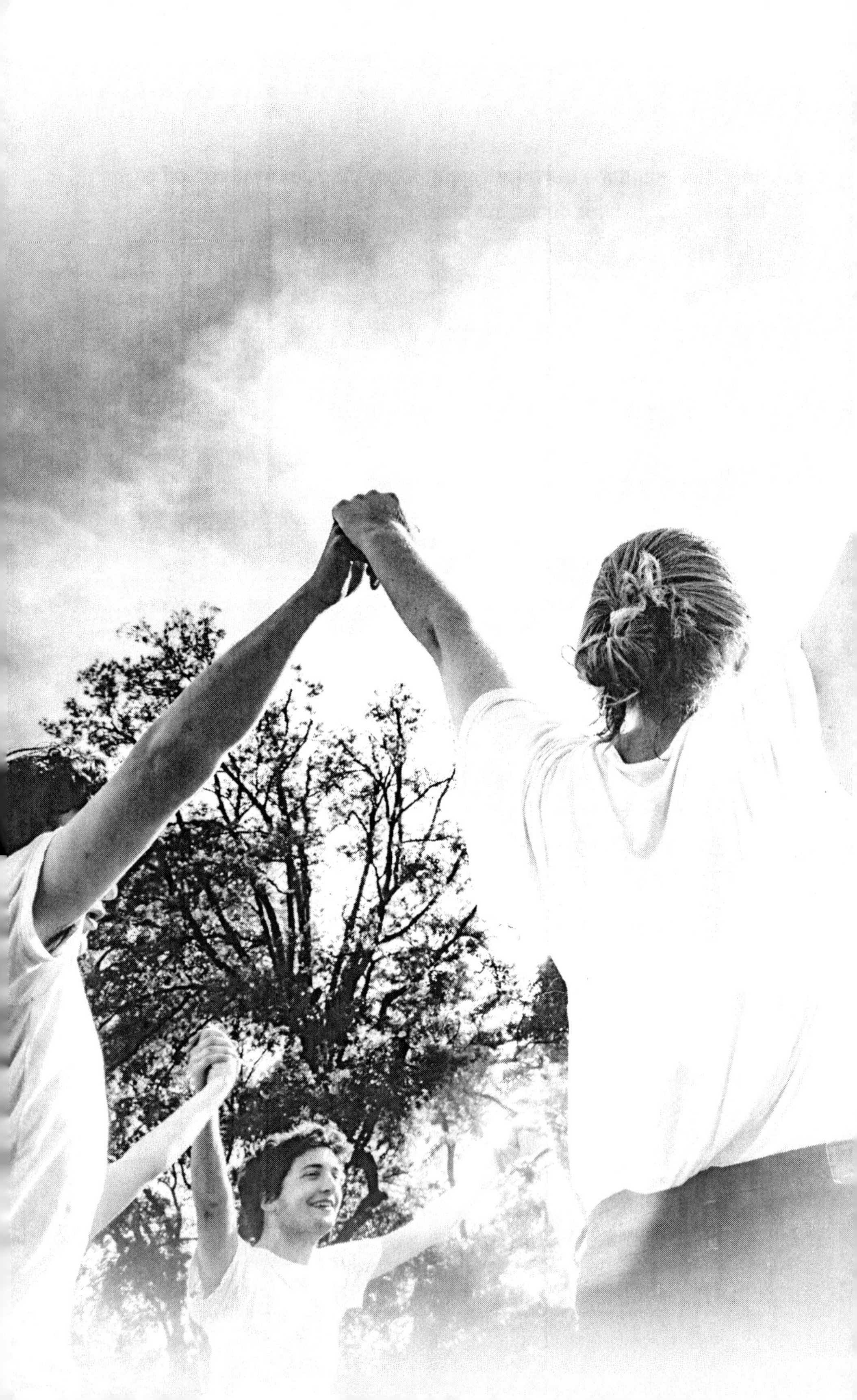

14

Father's Compassion

> "Biblical orthodoxy without compassion is surely the ugliest thing in the world." —Francis Schaeffer

We never know how our lives might impact those around us for their good. If we make ourselves available instruments of the Holy Spirit and become truly self-forgetful, our Father can express His heart to people in need around us. We call this "creative compassion," which simply models the heart of God to the world. The virgin birth of Christ was creative, His parables were creative, His miracles were creative, the cross as payment for our sin was creative, and His resurrection and ascension were creative. The Gospel is God reaching out to a broken world with audacious, creative compassion.

When God's creative compassion touches our lives, we are never the same. Our inward perspective begins to look outward. Rather than being self-absorbed, we become considerate of others. Where we used to be selfish and greedy, we are now open-handed and generous. These are all signs of finding the heart of our Father; we get to imitate His compassion for others. As pastor and author J.D. Greear has said, "Gospel change is the Spirit of God using the story of God to make the beauty of God come alive in our hearts"

The exercise of true compassion requires us to be close to hurting people. The word compassion at its root is a compound of two ideas: *suffer* and *together*. This means that when we express true compassion, we are in the lives of the hurting. It has us close to them, being where they live, seeing what they see, and feeling what they feel. Compassion, in its purest state, requires that we enter into the suffering of another at an emotional and practical level. Compassion is a feeling that moves us to act on behalf of someone in need. It goes beyond throwing rotten cabbage over the wall to feed "the under-privileged people" on the outside, to sitting with them and providing a meal suitable for our own table.

The prayer commonly known as the prayer of Saint Francis of Assisi, frames our heart's longing in simple but powerful words. Its first half reads:

> *"Lord, make me an instrument of thy peace.*
> *Where there is hatred, let me sow love;*
> *Where there is injury, pardon;*
> *Where there is doubt, faith;*
> *Where there is despair, hope;*
> *Where there is darkness, light;*
> *Where there is sadness, joy.*

Closely examining this prayer reveals the "places" compassion may take us to; places of hatred, injury, doubt, despair, darkness, and sadness. Do you still want to go? Creative compassion is willing to wade right into the messes of human depravity in order to bring the virtues of Jesus.

Compassion was powerfully modeled for us in the coming of Christ. The very word "incarnation" means *taking on flesh* and is used to describe how the eternal Son of God became human. The ultimate act of compassion was seen as the second person of the Trinity came in human flesh to "suffer with" us.

The Bible gives us another insight into what was required for Christ's incarnation. We see it in in Philippians 2 with the phrases "made himself nothing" and "emptied himself". The original Greek word used here is **"kenosis"** which speaks of Christ's 'self-emptying.' Jesus did not cease to be God in order to come to earth, but He did set aside His divine rights, privileges and glory to become like us. Again, we see in Jesus the embodiment of the Father's creative compassion.

Creative compassion is an attitude of emptying ourselves in order to be "Jesus with skin on" for one in need. The Message version of the Bible translates John 1:14 like this: *"The Word became flesh and blood, and moved into the neighborhood. We saw the glory with our own eyes, the one-of-a-kind glory, like Father, like Son, generous inside and out, true from start to finish."* This kind of compassion requires us to move in close enough so that we can touch people where they live.

The Jones kids saw the quiet and consistent lifestyle of creative compassion in their dad. He was graced, as all believers are, to move into people's lives with the love of God. Let's cross the Mexican border with Becky and her family to see how God powerfully used a simple gesture of kindness.

"The Power of a Peanut"

What a sight we must have been; Dad, a recent widower with his four daughters and Sharon, his sixteen-year-old niece, stuffed into our Ford Fairmont heading for Mexico. We were going to visit some special missionary friends, the Jepson's, in Tijuana. Our relationship became special through their many visits to our home over the years. The perk for our family during their annual ministry trip through our area, was that they parked their "motor home of wonders" in our driveway. Such a novelty to us kids! I spent a fair amount of time inconspicuously circling their home on wheels just hoping they'd see me and invite me in. Besides their cool teenage son, they always had at least three black poodles travelling with them. Mrs. Jepson showed us their dog's tricks and once in a while let us take them on walks. Mr. Jepson was funny, playful, and always making us laugh. He played the mandolin and taught us simple Sunday school songs in Spanish.

14: Father's Compassion – *"The Power of a Peanut"*

Though the Jepson's had been to our home many times, this would be the first time for us to visit them on their turf. In our eager anticipation of this adventure, my little sister Jodi and I played "going to Mexico" for weeks before our actual departure.

Besides being a favorite cousin, Sharon accompanied us on this trip to help Dad with the driving. We never considered it a problem that she was a newly licensed driver with little to no driving experience. Her crash course - thankfully minus the crash - involved navigating the narrow and winding roads of mountainous regions in the middle of the night while the rest of us slept like babies. I believe the most sincere prayers she ever prayed were the ones uttered from behind the wheel of that Ford Fairmont. Not being one to complain, we didn't learn how truly terrified she was in some of those situations until years later. By Sharon's testimony, the biggest miracle of the trip was getting there alive!

There was plenty to explore at the "Jepson rancho" - our name for the place in the boonies outside Tijuana where our missionary friends lived. Their motor home was like a castle compared to their simple

Journey to the Father

house in Mexico. We hunted rabbit for breakfast on the mountain behind their house. Grandma, who lived next door, had a parrot that drove the cat nearly crazy by incessantly calling, "here, kitty kitty."

The Jepson's invited Dad to preach at some small area churches. This was my first experience seeing Dad speak through a translator, and the first time us girls shared the Spanish choruses that Mr. Jepson had taught us back home, with people who actually understood the words. This was a fascinating place, and we hadn't even been to town yet!

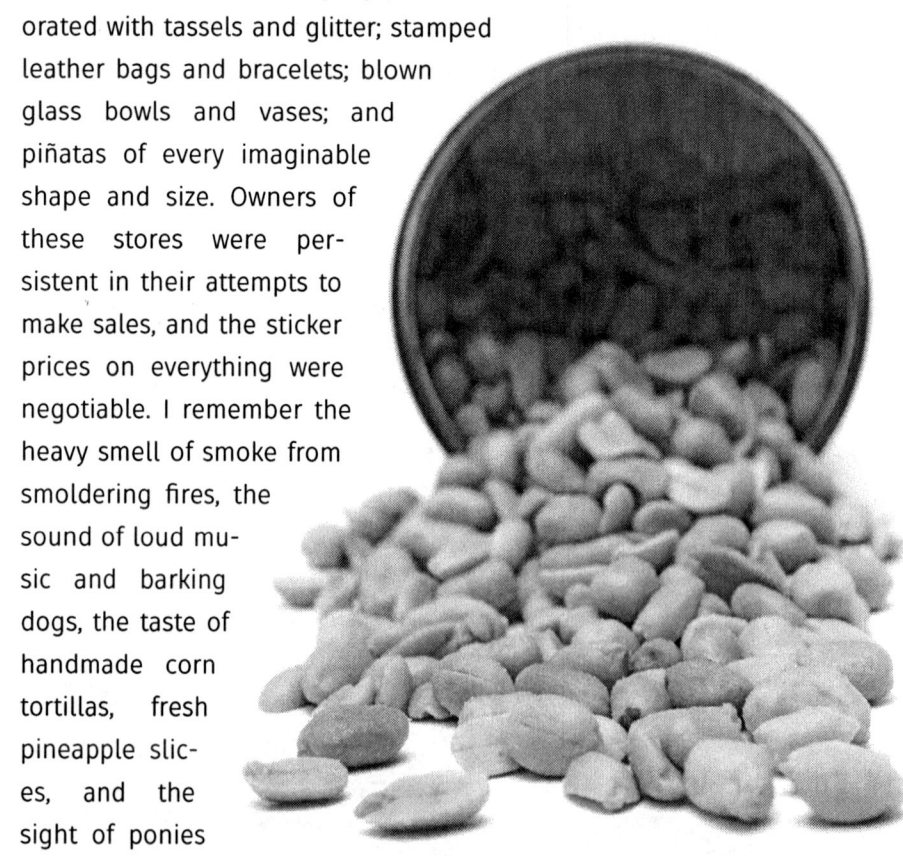

Downtown Tijuana made a lasting impression on me as a 9 year old, having never traveled beyond the borders of Midwestern USA before this. The narrow bustling streets were lined with stores with wide open doors, all carrying some variation of the same products; dresses and ponchos made of brightly patterned cloth; sombreros decorated with tassels and glitter; stamped leather bags and bracelets; blown glass bowls and vases; and piñatas of every imaginable shape and size. Owners of these stores were persistent in their attempts to make sales, and the sticker prices on everything were negotiable. I remember the heavy smell of smoke from smoldering fires, the sound of loud music and barking dogs, the taste of handmade corn tortillas, fresh pineapple slices, and the sight of ponies painted with black and white stripes to resemble zebras. For a small fee, you could sit on them, don a sombrero, and get your picture taken.

There were children everywhere. Most of them weren't wearing shoes and were trying to sell us something. They picked Dad out as a soft sell right away. Their assessment of his having low sales resistance was accurate, but their assumption of him being a rich gringo was not. His pockets were about as bare as theirs. That's when Dad spied the big can of peanuts. He purchased them in hopes of making some new friends. Dad's antics, especially with children, were always entertaining, but dealing with a language barrier took it to a whole new level. He waved, motioned, and signaled in an attempt to communicate his desire to share his peanuts with them. It was like a great game of charades. They approached cautiously and interacted shyly at first, but soon, a sea of beautiful, smiling, brown-faced kids surrounded us. Before long they were eating peanuts, laughing, and for a brief moment, forgetting their harsh and bleak existence.

We were going to miss a few days of school for this trip to Mexico. My 4th grade teacher's attempt at making this an educational experience encouraged me to keep a journal. It was a great idea, but I failed miserably. Here are my only two entries, both of which were penciled on the first day: "Well, we're off." And, "Iowa is very flat." That was the end of my journal entries, but thankfully not the end of my learning. I experienced a lot of firsts while south of the border; first time seeing and swimming in the ocean; first time picking and eating an orange right off the tree; first time climbing a mountain; first time breaking a piñata. But the first I cherish most is the memory of sharing a snack with children in downtown Tijuana. It didn't make it into my journal, but the lesson remains with me to this day:

Sometimes the greatest impact is made through the smallest gesture. Never under estimate the power of a peanut!

One might be quick to dismiss "the power of a peanut," but in the hands of the right person, it can draw a crowd and express Christ's love. Don't let the term "creative compassion" put you off if you don't consider yourself a creative person. In fact, most acts of this nature are quite simple. Consider the parable that Jesus told about the end of the age when the Father calls His sheep before His heavenly throne. Notice this gripping portion of the story in Matthew 25:34-40

"Then the King will say to those on his right, 'Come, you who are blessed by my Father; take your inheritance, the kingdom prepared for you since the creation of the world. For I was hungry and you gave me something to eat, I was thirsty and you gave me something to drink, I was a stranger and you invited me in, I needed clothes and you clothed me, I was sick and you looked after me, I was in prison and you came to visit me.'

"Then the righteous will answer him, 'Lord, when did we see you hungry and feed you, or thirsty and give you something to drink? When did we see you a stranger and invite you in, or needing clothes and clothe you? When did we see you sick or in prison and go to visit you?'

"The King will reply, 'Truly I tell you, whatever you did for one of the least of these brothers and sisters of mine, you did for me.'"

If we live our lives expressing ordinary acts of compassion toward those around us, we will be among those to the right of the King in this story who are blessed and rewarded by the Father. There is nothing flashy about these gracious acts listed by the Lord. Have you ever helped someone by providing a meal, a drink, or some clothing? Have you ever had someone stay in your home because they needed a place of refuge? Have you ever assisted someone who was ill or visited someone in jail? There is really nothing glamorous about any of these acts, yet, when they are done in Jesus' name, they become more powerful than we can imagine. In a reply of true self-forgetfulness, these blessed ones told the King that they had no memory of serving Him in this way.

14: Father's Compassion – *"The Power of the Peanut"*

Then in a strange and surprising twist, the King announces that when they compassionately served these needy people, they were actually serving HIM! He was that homeless guy. He was that desperately broken woman. He was the prisoner behind bars. He was the young college student stranded along the road with a flat tire. He was the one ministered to in all those, now forgotten, acts of creative compassion. Even if you only have a jar of peanuts, God can use YOU!

Get in the Story:

1. Reread the prayer of Saint Francis of Assisi. Ask the Lord to open your eyes to see the troubled places where He would call you to bring His compassion.

    "Lord, make me an instrument of thy peace.
    Where there is hatred, let me sow love;
    Where there is injury, pardon;
    Where there is doubt, faith;
    Where there is despair, hope;
    Where there is darkness, light;
    Where there is sadness, joy.

2. What might your own *"kenosis"* (self-emptying) look like as you move toward others in compassion?

3. Of the six specific acts of compassion named in the parable of Matthew 25: 34-40, are there any you have not yet participated in? How can you increase your impact?

14: Father's Compassion – *"The Power of the Peanut"*

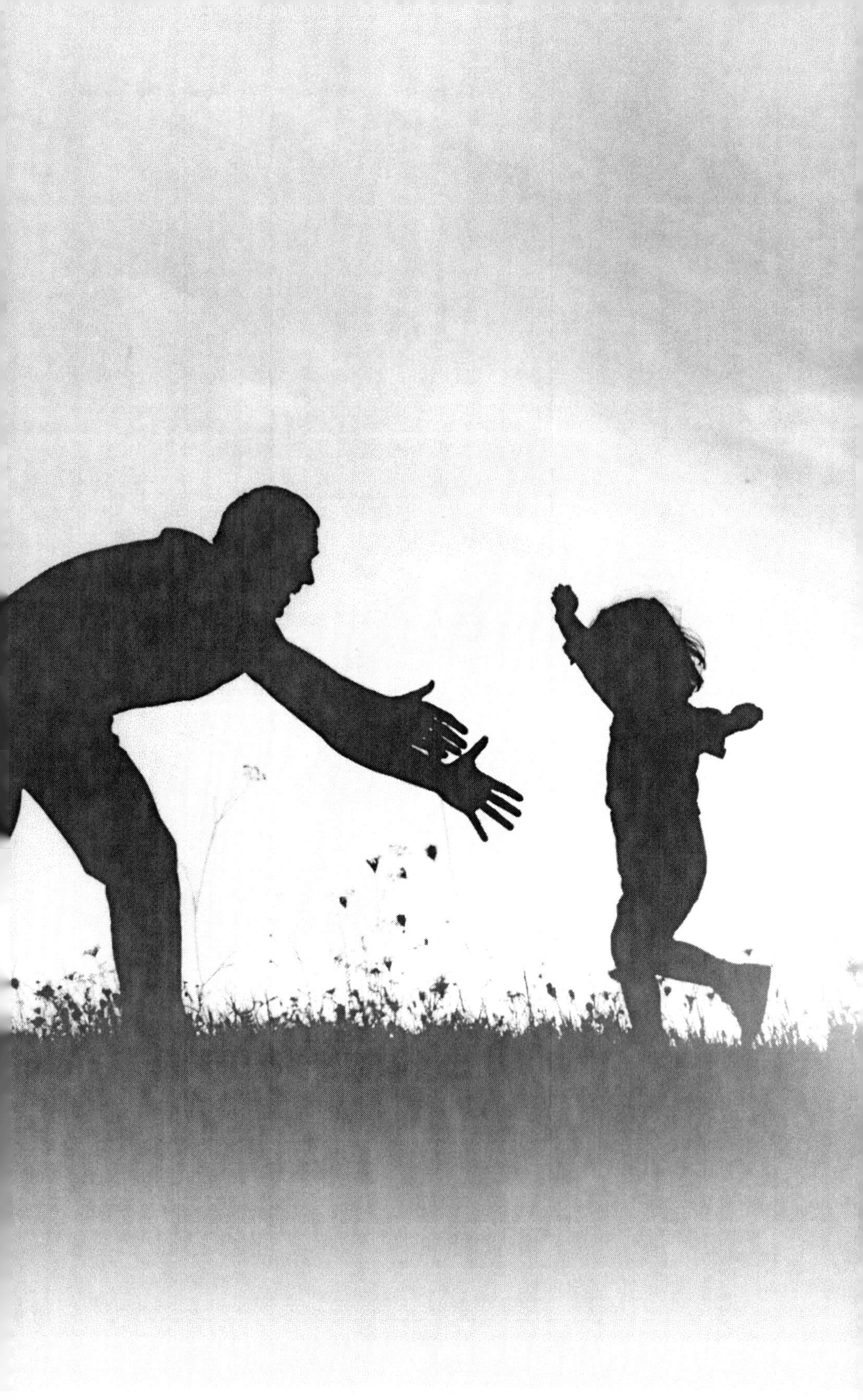

15

Father's Patience

> "If you took the love of all the best mothers and fathers who ever lived (think about that for a moment) — all the goodness, kindness, patience, fidelity, wisdom, tenderness, strength and love — and united all those virtues in one person, that person would only be a faint shadow of the love and mercy in the heart of God for you and me."
> —Brennan Manning

Jesus taught the great spiritual truths of the Kingdom using parables. A parable is an earthly story with a heavenly meaning. One of these timeless and familiar stories, about the prodigal son, reveals some significant things about the father heart of God.

We read this story of a father and his two sons in Luke 15. The younger son, in rebellion, wanted to receive his father's inheritance early and leave home, while the older son was content to stay at home and continue working diligently. We often focus on the younger son as the one being far away from his father's heart, but it is actually true of both sons. The younger is separated because of sin and shame, and the older because of self-righteousness and pride. They were, in fact, *both* prodigal sons. The younger son distanced himself from his father's abundance by running far away, the older son, remained at a distance from all his father desired to give him without ever leaving home. Both ended up living like slaves and paupers. They each represent the two places many Christians live in their relationship to Father God.

For all the drama of the two sons, this parable reveals much about the father's heart as well. In the story, we see the father's consistent love for his sons, even through their waywardness. Notice that he seems to keep watch on the road for the return of his younger son. Verse 20 reads, *"But while he was still a long way off, his father saw him and was filled with compassion for him; he ran to his son, threw his arms around him and kissed him."* A little further into the story, we see the father's extravagant favor toward the older son, who was angry and resentful over the celebration of his younger brother's return. Verse 31 says, *"My son, you are always with me, and everything I have is yours."* Both sons learned about the true heart of their father that day. Both were given the invitation to the party of ultimate restoration. At times we are deceived and rebellious like the younger son. Other times, in our struggle with self-righteousness and hard-hearted arrogance, we more closely resemble the older son. Just as the father in the story related to his sons, so our Heavenly Father relates to us with unrelenting love and abundant grace in order to release us from our wayward hearts.

The term "prodigal" is usually used to describe someone who is wayward, but the word actually means extravagant, lavish, unrestrained; even to the point of being wasteful. Ironically, this word better describes the father in the parable, revealing the reckless, unrestrained, extravagant love of our Father God toward us!

"You're a Good Kid!"

I can't explain how it happened. I woke up one morning around age 15, and everything Dad did drove me nuts. I can't remember a time when he didn't welcome the morning with singing, yet all of a sudden each word he sang was now a sour note in my ears. His once appreciated affection suddenly made my skin crawl. Any glance from him in my direction sent me heading off in the opposite one. It wasn't that I stopped loving him; I just temporarily couldn't stand him.

There was no mistaking the pain and concern in his eyes as this stage continued. For two years he *saw* me on a regular basis, but he didn't hear much from me at all. I acted "normal" around others, but barely acknowledged his existence. My sisters, youth leaders, and friends became my confidants. I gave them the luxury of my words, but left Dad with the impossible task of decoding my confusing and ever-fluctuating moods. If something great or disappointing happened in my life, he was the last to hear about it, and it was usually from someone other than me. I didn't like myself for it and resolved with prayer and determination to respond differently. Yet, I seemed to remain helplessly stuck in the gear of adolescent aversion to parents.

Thank goodness dad was stuck in another gear... the gear of unrelenting love. "You're a good kid, Beck" was his constant affirmation. A good kid? Are you kidding? I was obnoxious and rude! How could he say that? His response left me with yet another dilemma: how was I supposed to receive love when punishment is what I deserved? I found that downright irritating, then again, everything Dad did irritated me at that time.

Receiving affirmation is relatively easy to take when we believe we deserve it, but to receive it when we don't is usually our undoing. It certainly was mine. As my high school years ended and my college years began, something amazing occurred. All of a sudden my Dad began acquiring wisdom! (Isn't it amazing how parents in this stage of our lives undergo a magical transformation from ignorant to ingenious?) In reality, it was my attitude, not Dad that began to change. My heart opened to him once again, slowly but sincerely. I *felt* drawn toward him long before I was willing to demonstrate it with words or actions. He was patient with my return; warmly receiving, but not overly-expecting my affection. By God's grace, and Dad's unwavering acceptance, coinciding with a little maturity finally kicking in on my end, our relationship was restored. It wasn't long before I was missing him terribly, and not hesitating to tell him so.

Many years have passed since then. Trusting the transforming power of unrelenting love, my Dad chose to affirm my identity instead of my behavior. He loved me for being, not just for doing. Dad's love didn't diminish when my love for him waned. I moved; I wandered, and he stood steadfastly patient, in loving, redemptive hope.

My need for this kind of love didn't end with adolescence. Many times since then, I have needed this type of love; with a wandering child and as a waiting parent. Apart from God's unrelenting, unconditional love, my resistance to Him would have kept me eternally stuck.

Our Heavenly Father initiates, we respond. His love never fails!

It's easy to appear "normal" on the outside while harboring unforgiveness or resentment on the inside. Our relationships with others, for the most part, carry on as usual, while the relationship with our Heavenly Father suffers. We feel distanced from God just like Becky did from her dad. We may feel He has withdrawn His love from us, when all the while we're the ones pushing Him away. We are confounded by the reality of His unrelenting love for us even in our rebellion against Him. *"If we are faithless, he remains faithful, for he cannot disown himself."*- 2 Timothy 2:13

God initiated His love toward us and enabled our becoming His children. We were born guilty of sin. Not only did He withhold the punishment we deserved, He took the punishment upon Himself! *"God made Him who had no sin to be sin for us, so that in Him we might become the righteousness of God."*-1 Corinthians 5:21 Did you catch the new identity spelled out for us in this Scripture? Through Him we go from being "sinners in a heap of trouble" to being *"the righteousness of God in Christ!"* When God looks at His children, He sees His Son. Do you remember what God spoke from heaven over Jesus at his baptism? *"This is my son, whom I love; with Him I am well pleased."* Our Heavenly Father speaks that same affirmation over His children today. In essence He's saying, "You're a good kid."

> "Though the mountains be shaken and the hills be removed, yet my unfailing love for you will not be shaken nor my covenant of peace be removed." —Isaiah 54:10

In the parable of the Prodigal Son, the father sees the wayward younger son from a long way off. He stood daily looking down the road in hopeful expectation of his son's return. One day he saw a dark figure of a man on the horizon. Was it just another traveler? As he came closer the father continued to stare. "Could it be?" Now approaching the outer gate, the father recognizes his wayward child. "My son!" With that, he takes off running and embraces the estranged and emaciated boy in a tight, spinning hug of overflowing joy!

Our Father still fixes His gaze longingly in our direction when we go astray. When we return, he embraces us with delight, not condemnation. He even goes beyond that and throws us a party. *"Quick! Bring the best robe and put it on him. Put a ring on his finger and sandals on his feet. Bring the fattened calf and kill it. Let's have a feast and celebrate. For this son of mine was dead and is alive again; he was lost and is found."* (Luke 15:22-24) The real message of this story is the ecstatic response of our loving Father to a wayward son or daughter coming home. When we return to Him in humble repentance, He meets us with grace and mercy. Author and pastor, Max Lucado puts it this way, "The difference between mercy and grace? Mercy gave the prodigal son a second chance. Grace gave him a feast." The act of the father giving the son the best robe, the ring, and sandals all speaks of our Lord's lavish love and of His generous reconciling grace. The status of "sonship" is unquestionably restored.

> "But you, Lord, are a compassionate and gracious God, slow to anger, abounding in love and faithfulness." —Psalm 86:15

And what about the Father's heart toward his dutiful older son? Favor. Acceptance. Generosity. *"...everything I have is yours."* (Luke 15:31b) How sad that the son's resentment kept him from receiving the fullness of his father's love. There is no room for celebration in the heart of one who insists on working for what can only be freely received. We read in Luke 15:29-30, the older son's angry response to his father's pleading for his participation in his younger brother's welcome home party: *"Look! All these years I've been slaving for you and never disobeyed your orders. Yet you never gave me even a young goat so I could celebrate with my friends. But when this son of yours who has squandered your property with prostitutes comes home, you kill the fattened calf for him!"*

Like the elder brother in the parable, we are often inclined to withhold a lavish reception for the sinner-come-home. This subtle attitude of "withholding favor" is perhaps especially true in our relationships that are closest to home. Something within us feels justified to require a bit of groveling from the prodigal, or for them to be placed on monitored probation to confirm their repentance. We take offense when a wrongdoer is shown mercy. Sadly, this exacting attitude causes us to miss out on many of God's celebrations, not to mention all the juicy slices of grilled "fattened calf" on our party plate!

A dear friend of ours was teaching his son how to drive. The son had taken drivers training and was confident in his knowledge of the rules of the road. He had his learners permit and was out with his dad, glad to be behind the wheel and getting some driving practice. He was approaching an intersection with traffic lights to make a left hand turn. The green arrow indicated he was legally permitted to make this maneuver. The only problem was, at the same time that he was heading into his turn, there was a car coming straight through the intersection from the opposite direction. His dad yelled, "stop," and they just barely avoided a head-on collision! After their adrenaline normalized, our friend asked his son what in the world he was thinking by pulling out in front of oncoming traffic. His son said, "Dad, I had the right of way!" His dad's reply was simple, straightforward, and profound. "Son, you can be right... and dead!" This comes to my mind every time I think of the older brother in the parable of the prodigal son. He stayed at home working diligently for his father while his younger brother was out sowing his wild oats. He was doing everything right, but was in many ways "dead."

Becky and her dad endured some confusing and painful years of strained distance between them. Denver stood steadfast in his love for her while her heart was closed to him. He sought comfort from his Father and prayed, trusting His reach to exceed what he could not grasp. Her return would be God's doing, not his. *"Being confident of this, that he who began a good work in you will carry it on to completion until the day of Christ Jesus."* Philippians 1:6 When there was little he could do to change her behavior, he reinforced her status in his eyes, "You're a good kid, Beck," which affirmed her identity in Christ—You are loved. This is our standing before our

Journey to the Father

Heavenly Father. His boundless love makes Him act with recklessly unrestrained love, grace, and mercy toward us.

Get into the Story:

1. Of the two brothers in the parable of the Prodigal Son (Luke 15), which one can you relate to most? Why?

2. The sins of either overt rebellion or inward self-righteousness work to destroy our true spiritual identity. Consider how the Father's unrelenting love has helped you find restoration as a beloved, favored part of His family.

_____

_____

_____

_____

_____

_____

_____

_____

3. Are you standing in the place of the father, waiting longingly and looking to the horizon for the return of a wayward son or daughter? Receive the comfort of your Father's love and freshly entrust your loved one to Him.

_____

_____

_____

_____

_____

_____

_____

_____

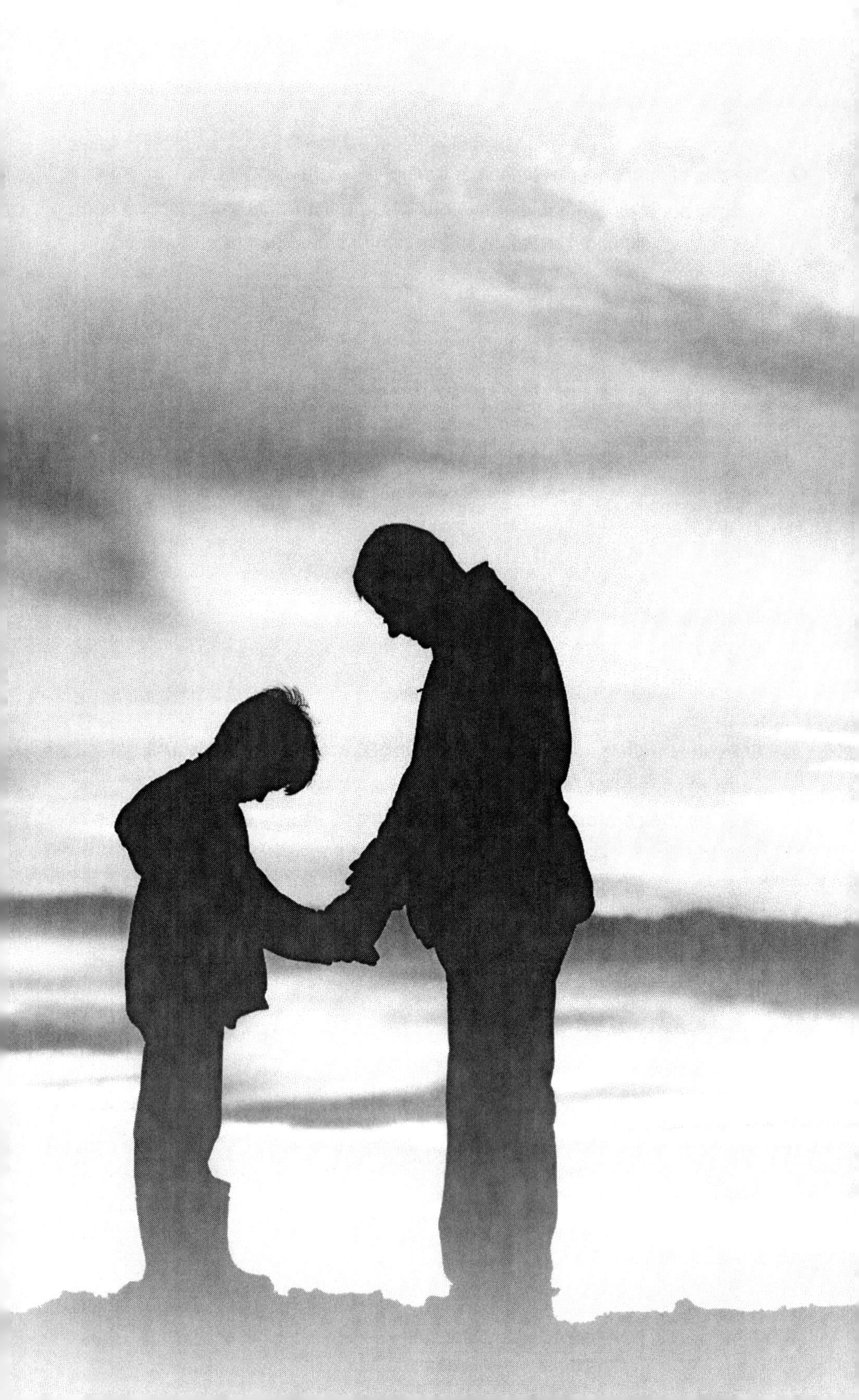

16

Father's Forgiveness

> "We must develop and maintain the capacity to forgive. He who is devoid of the power to forgive is devoid of the power to love. There is some good in the worst of us and some evil in the best of us. When we discover this, we are less prone to hate our enemies."
>
> —Martin Luther King, Jr.

Offense happens. Sounds like a bumper sticker, doesn't it? If it were, there would be none truer. It may be overt or subtle, deliberate or unintentional, major or insignificant. It may come through someone close to us or through someone we've never met, but it will happen. Sooner or later, all of us will we be wronged, misrepresented, overlooked, misunderstood, insulted, criticized, disagreed with; well, you get the idea. Offense happens, but what happens when we're offended? This is where we have some options. How we respond to the inevitability of offense has immense implications, either positively or negatively. When we choose to follow the Good Shepherd, we may think that life will be all still waters and green pastures, but in David's 23rd Psalm, there is also mention of valleys full of death shadows.

We successfully navigate both of these terrains by holding tight to the Father's hand. Offense will touch every life, and though it has the potential to destroy us, it is also has the power to transform us.

When people hurt us, on purpose or not, we are prone to react with any number of emotions: anger, rage, disappointment, depression, aggression and resentment, to name a few. The fact is, rejection hurts deeply. We are not disembodied spirits, void of feeling. Nor are we to be spiritual Pollyanna's, thinking that because we're Christians, this kind of relational pain won't touch us. With the high ideals of Jesus as our guide and the love of God as our aim, what could go wrong, right? Enter our sin and yet-to-be-fully-sanctified-human-nature. Relational wounding in the body of Christ is often the most painful of all. Relational tensions are not new to us as Jesus-followers. The Lord's disciples, as well as those who faithfully served the early church felt their sting. *"I entreat Euodia and I entreat Syntyche to agree in the Lord. Yes, I ask you also, true companion, help these women, who have labored side by side with me in the gospel."* Philippians 4:2-3a (ESV)

When offended, we can feel justified in our position. However, Jesus doesn't casually suggest we forgive those who offend us; He commands it. (Matthew 6:14) He knows the devastating effects of unforgiveness and loves us too much to give us the option. When we carry resentment and unforgiveness, the divine flow of God's Spirit is stifled among us. It is only in unity that the fullness of the Holy Spirit flows freely (Psalm 133 and Acts 2:42-47). The Apostle Paul set a high bar for the well-taught church in Ephesus, where he ministered for three years. *"And do not grieve the Holy Spirit of God, with whom you were sealed for the day of redemption. Get rid of all bitterness, rage and anger, brawling and slander, along with every form of malice. Be kind and compassionate to one another, forgiving each other, just as in Christ, God forgave you."* Ephesians 4:30-32 That Scripture passage ends with seven very powerful words; "just as in Christ God forgave you." Jesus is commanding us to do nothing more than what He first modeled for us by His great forgiveness!

16: Father's Forgiveness – *"Offense-Free Living"*

"Offense-Free Living"

In the later years of Dad's life, I reflected to him what I considered to be one of the greatest gifts he had given me: modeling an offense-free life. I didn't realize that living *without* offense was a rare or unique quality until I saw the devastation it created in the lives of people who had lived *with* it. I also saw the uncomely fruit of unforgiveness and bitterness that sprang up in my own heart. Offense is as natural to the human heart as breathing is to the body. We don't have to go looking for opportunities to get offended because they present themselves to us on a regular basis. So, what was Dad's secret? It wasn't that the opportunity for offense never came knocking; he just refused to let it take root in his heart. I observed in him what I called an "unclogged wellspring", and I came to understand it was the result of a well-guarded heart. *Above all else, guard your heart, for everything you do flows from it.* —Proverbs 4:23. What flowed from his life was sweet because his "well" was clean. His well was clean because he had been diligent to guard his heart. He was able to guard his heart because of the magnificent grace of God.

It is a challenge to capture the particulars of how Dad's life displayed this beautiful grace. It is only as I look back from the vantage point of adulthood that I truly see how hurtful and painful some of Dad's life experiences must have been. When they unfolded in real time, he never made mention of them. When he spoke of them after the fact, it was always in the light of redemption. "Life's difficulties can make us either bitter or better", was one of Dad's common sayings. The following stories give a peek into some of the choices he was presented with and the decisions he made which formed the man he would become.

In 1971, when Dad was still grieving the loss of his wife to cancer, and while raising five kids as a single dad, a minister from India visited our fledgling church. He had a compelling testimony, a charismatic personality, and came on the recommendation of people Dad knew and trusted. He stayed longer than anyone had planned and began drawing people to himself. As Dad began to regain emotional and spiritual strength, he discerned something very unhealthy going on with how this man was relating to the church. Long story short, he hijacked the flock, leading some of them into what became a full-blown cult. Most of these dear deceived people never spiritually recovered. Dad was disillusioned. Had he failed God? How could the sheep under his watch be led into such extreme levels of deception? Had his reputation and witness for Christ been tarnished? Would God ever trust him to lead His people again?

Dad's British background most often curried favor, but once in a while it worked against him in the church setting. He skated on thin ice when wading into current events, like the time he went on about his concern over Marilyn Monroe trying to take prayer out of public schools. He of course meant to say Madalyn Murray O'hair, but the names just got confused in his mind. When he misspoke, his accent sometimes saved him. Such was the case in this instance. Another time, however, the implication of his being from another country was not so humorous. Dad was pastoring a church on an interim basis after the former pastor, who was also his best friend, had died. Dad was engaged to be married to this man's widow, and although their relationship was pure, some church members were suspect of something scandalous going on. Dad was out on visitation one afternoon and happened to stop at the home of a family from church where the wife was leading a bible study. He was invited in during a discussion involving the daughter of one of the parishioners. The daughter had gone to a square dance and the women were in disagreement about whether or not square dancing was acceptable in the eyes of God. Dad, having no clue as to what a square dance was asked them to enlighten him. As far as he could understand, it was what in his country was called a folk dance. Folk dances in Wales were a cultural tradition. He saw nothing improper about that sort of thing and offered his humble opinion. Not long after that incident, it was time for the annual church business meeting with the entire congregation in attendance. Dad didn't care for business meetings as much as he did prayer meetings, but he attended for the fellowship factor. He had no idea he was about to come under fire. He was shocked, not to mention very confused, when three deacons accused him of planning to hold wild dance parties in the church basement. This rumor had grown out of the square dancing discussion at the ladies bible study. It took more than fellowship and good coffee to redeem that business meeting. Dad, who had become the subject of gossip, was misjudged, and wrongly accused. It had to be hurtful. Should he defend himself, become distrustful of people, and close his heart off to future relationships?

In the early 80's, Dad was invited to pastor a group forming a new church in Southern Minnesota. He and my step-mom Dianne felt the Lord leading in this direction, so they willingly went. A lot of spiritual formation and practical organization was needed. God's grace was upon them, and they experienced steady and healthy growth. By year three, the spirit of unity was tested. The murmuring and grumbling among some of the flock sent spiritual tremors through the church. Something was about to blow. One Sunday morning as church was getting ready to start, a loud and obviously agitated Deacon approached Dad with an issue that had clearly been brewing in him for a long time. His confrontation ended with an ultimatum. "Denver, either you leave or I'm leaving!" God had not indicated that Dad's time pastoring this church was done, so he informed the man that until he heard otherwise, he was saying put. With that, the deacon gathered his family and stormed out, never to return. How's that for an opener to worship? Dad had been disrespected, insulted, embarrassed; and all before having to deliver a sermon! Was this deacon expressing what everyone else was thinking? Would he loose heart and leave even though he felt God wanted him to stay?

Another time, Dad was at his sister's flat in London after making the long trip to visit his beloved homeland. It was his first stop after many hours of travel on planes, trains, and automobiles. He had planned to stay with her for a couple of days before going to spend the rest of his time with the family in Wales. He arrived later than expected and hadn't called to let her know. This was before we had the luxury of cell phones. He wearily walked to her place from the train station, sustained by the anticipation of seeing his sister. She was visibly upset when she met him at the door. Sympathetic to her feelings he apologized profusely for being late, thinking they'd both feel much better after a hot cup of tea. Unfortunately, he never got his cup of tea. In fact, he never made it inside the house. She said if that's the way he was going to treat her, he wasn't welcome to stay. Dejected and crestfallen, he slowly turned around and walked away. How was he going to respond to rejection from his own family? Would his relationship with his sister ever be restored?

In each of these extremely difficult situations, no doubt, Dad experienced an onslaught of negative emotions and fought hard to keep his head straight and his heart right. He did not walk through these experiences perfectly, but He did so humbly. By the grace of God, he made the choice to forgive himself, God, and others, again and again.

16: Father's Forgiveness – "Offense-Free Living"

Evidently there is no room for offense in a heart occupied by forgiveness. I cannot recall one instance where Dad cast people or God's church in a bad light. When he spoke *to* people or *about* people, his words affirmed their value. He was the same at home as behind the pulpit. Instead of blaming, he took responsibility for what he had the ability to change – himself. Instead of feeling like a victim, he let God be his Victor. He didn't deny the harsh realities of life circumstances, but received God's grace in the midst of them. The Lord was his Shepherd, not leading him *around,* but faithfully *through* the deep valleys of disappointment, discouragement, deceit, disillusionment, distraction, detours, and disasters.

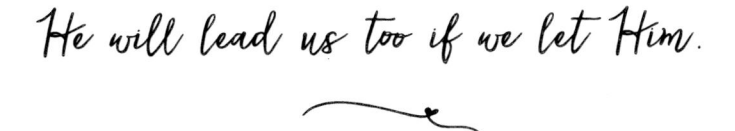

He will lead us too if we let Him.

Your life journey is like driving down a highway. You are cruising along just fine when all of a sudden you see an offense approaching at high speed. Just then you notice an off ramp with a sign that says grace. You have a choice to make: keep going straight and run right into the offense, or take the exit of grace and miss it. This is the picture in Hebrews 12:15. *"See to it that no one misses the grace of God and that no bitter root grows up to cause trouble and defile many."* Did you notice the costly damages that are incurred when we don't take the escape route God provided and instead let offense crash into our lives? A bitter root grows up and *many* are defiled (tainted, corrupted, and ruined). Our unwillingness to forgive always affects more than just ourselves.

The only way we can live offense-free lives is to regularly consider how much God, in Christ, has forgiven us. Look at the powerful grace displayed in Christ as he went to his death on a brutal Roman cross. While they were driving the nails in His hands, He prayed for them, *"Father, forgive them, for they do not know what they are doing"* Luke 23:34. Walking in this kind of forgiveness is not only counterintuitive, but impossible for the unredeemed soul. Our inclination is to react with hate and get revenge. But He audaciously commands the redeemed to love, do good to, bless, and pray for our enemies. *"But to you who are listening I say: Love your enemies, do good to those who hate you, bless those who curse you, pray for those who mistreat you."* Luke 6:27-28. Notice that Jesus' command is not conditional on whether or not our enemies repent and apologize for their transgression. We are called to forgive even if the wrongdoer is never sorry for their offense. This does not diminish in any way the wrong they did, but it relieves the one who was wronged from the burden of having to manage the punishment of their offender.

When it comes to forgiveness, we cannot out give God. Think of it this way: you are a successful billionaire working in downtown New York City. As you step out of your taxi to pay the driver, you accidentally drop a $10.00 bill and it blows down the street and across the lanes of fast-moving traffic. Would you risk your life chasing down that bill? Would you feel like your life was ruined because you just lost ten bucks? No, you'd shrug it off and move on...no big deal, there is plenty more where that came from. Now, let's say you're a Christian. If we lay awake at night because someone mistreated us, we're acting like a billionaire down on his hands and knees looking for a $10.00 bill. We have the approval of heaven and have been forgiven of every sin by the Father, yet we obsess over a $10.00 offense. Let's not forget that God has opened up a bank account of grace with our name on it. We can withdraw the riches we've been given in Christ, forgive the wrongdoer, let it go and move on!

When a root of bitterness is allowed to grow it has the potential to *defile* many, just as a well-guarded heart that draws on the grace of God to forgive will *bless* many. When offense came Denver's way, he chose to take the exit of grace, and as a result, lived out his days with a radiant joy. The same can be true of us as we continually choose to forgive and live free from offense.

16: Father's Forgiveness – *"Offense-Free Living"*

Get into the Story:

1. Think of a time when you were hurt, insulted or offended by someone. What were some of the emotions you wrestled with?

_____

_____

_____

_____

_____

_____

_____

_____

2. Hebrews 12:15 tells us to not miss the grace of God and allow a bitter root to spring up. Has there ever been a time when you noticed a bitter root and had to go back to dig it out of your life?

_____

_____

_____

_____

_____

_____

Journey to the Father

3. Is there someone you need to forgive from your heart? If so, make a withdrawal on God's grace and truly forgive, releasing them from all judgment. Remember, forgiveness is a decision not a feeling. Write out a specific prayer of forgiveness and blessing over your offender.

16: Father's Forgiveness – *"Offense-Free Living"*

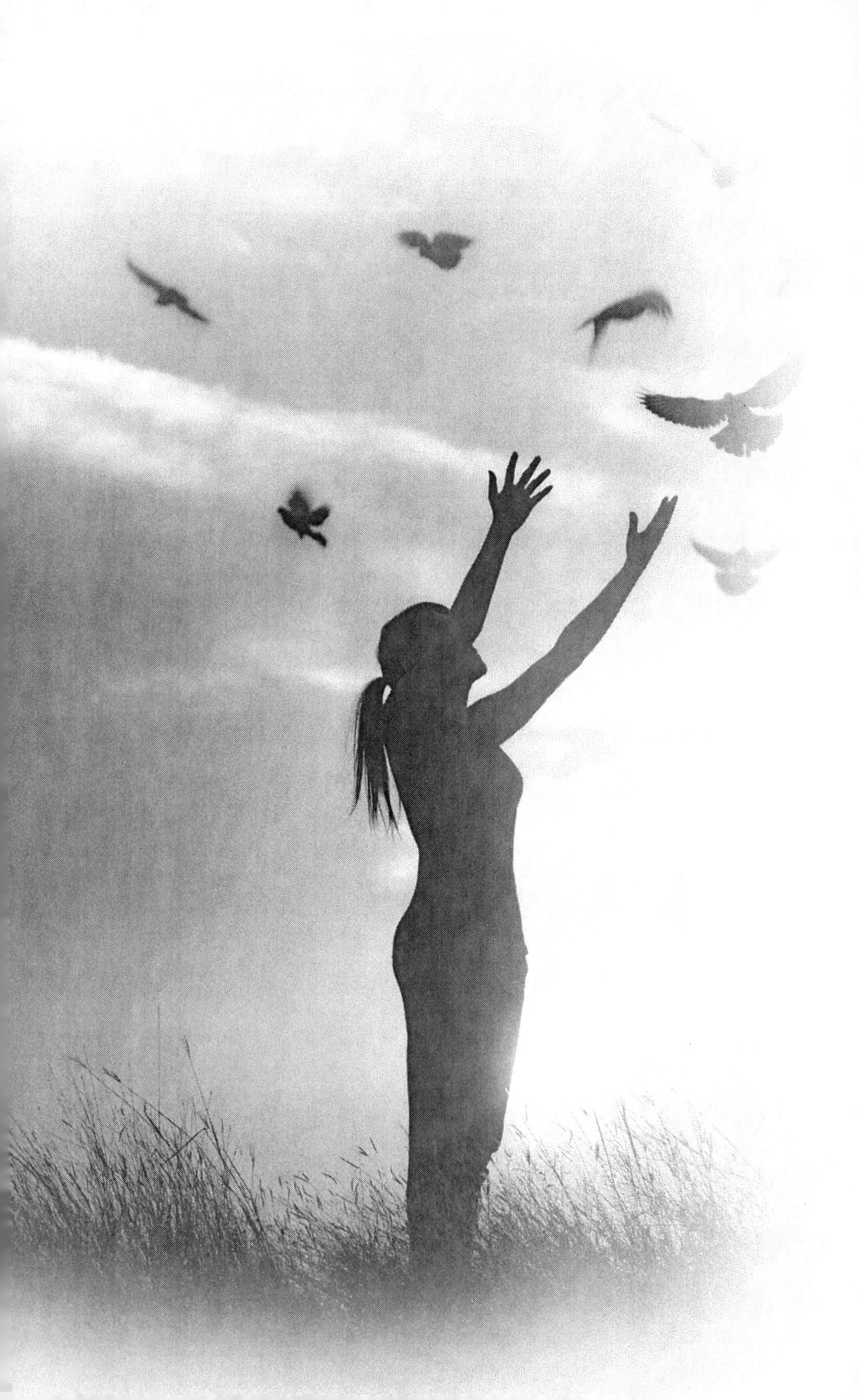

17

Father's Love

> "The presence of fear does not mean you have no faith. Fear visits everyone. But make your fear a visitor and not a resident." —Max Lucado

In the moment of facing our greatest fear, we are presented with an opportunity to be delivered from it. This was Becky's surprising experience when confronted with a fear she couldn't outrun. Her mom's death was traumatic in many ways, but one event from that experience was especially terrifying to 7-year-old Becky. Her mom had died at home in the night. By the time Denver shared the news of Dorothy's death with the kids the next morning, her body had already been taken away. The next time the family saw their mother was at the funeral home. The family approached the casket for a private moment together. Everyone except Becky found it a necessary and helpful time of closure and could have benefited by lingering for a little while. Becky, however, requested to leave immediately. The visual image of her mom's lifeless body was imprinted in her mind and struck terror in her heart

For many years after that experience she struggled intensely with a dead body phobia. You can imagine that this made for some awkward moments during our time of pastoral ministry - there were a lot of funerals to attend over those thirty years. Becky resolutely battled this inner trepidation, experiencing both victories and setbacks along the way. We prayed together often before funerals and visitation services. I [Sonny], would often ask during these occasions, "Becky, how are you doing?" Once, in a nervous attempt to lighten the situation, she revealed her secret strategy of viewing the deceased without fainting: "I just don't make eye contact!" Becky fought this phobia on into her adult years, trusting that God wanted her free. In the words of Pastor Rick Warren, "Fear is a self imposed prison that will keep you from becoming what God intends for you to be. You must move against it with the weapons of faith and love."

We later learned that the phobia Becky lived with is quite common when a child has lost a loved one. Death is just one trauma among myriads that can grip a child's heart with fear. Without complete healing, the terrors of childhood follow us on into adulthood. However, it is God's full intention to deliver us from fear. When we seek the Lord, even as children, He will show us the root lie in our fear and graciously help us replace it with His truth. *"I sought the Lord, and he answered me; he delivered me from all my fears."* —Psalm 34:4

It is commonly said that, "Fear is the darkroom where all of our negatives are developed." While certainly true, it is wise to discern between our valid and invalid fears. While *rational* fear is helpful, as in keeping us from stepping off the edge of a cliff, nothing good comes out of *irrational* fear. And what about this "darkroom" in the above phrase? While it has the potential to develop what is negative, walking through a dark place might also drive us into the arms of our Father as never before. Could the virtues of light, freedom, and truth come from our time in the "darkroom?" In his famous poem, *"The Dark Night,"* 16th-century Spanish poet and Roman Catholic mystic, Saint John of the Cross, extols the graces that can be added to our lives through a dark night of the soul:

O, night thou was my guide!
O, night more loving than the rising sun!
O, night that joined the Lover to the beloved one!
Transforming each of them into the other.

—St. John of the Cross

Darkness can join us to the Lover of our soul and be the vehicle to a new level of transformation. Facing the gloom of death is a battle we instinctively fight, but what if rather than wading into the battle alone and ending up blinded by the inky blackness of fear, we chose to cling to the One in Whom no darkness dwells. When we follow Him into our dreaded night we find it is where He shines the brightest. *"Even the darkness will not be dark to you; the night will shine like the day, for darkness is as light to you."* —Psalm 139:12

"Perfect Love Drives out Fear"

"Dad, I'm scared!" My dad heard this from me in the middle of the night on a regular basis for many years after mom passed away. I was seven years old when mom died at home, at night. Loosing dad in the same manner, or in any manner, became my greatest fear. Dad's response to my nearly nightly mantra was always the same: he'd scoop me up next to him, pray for me, and remind me of what the Bible says: *"Perfect love drives out fear."* I'd settle in under his "wing" and eventually fall back asleep.

Thirty years later, I found myself at his bedside, facing my greatest fear. Dad had been in a car accident that left him in a shallow coma. We were given the gift of twelve days following the accident to be with him before he passed away. Though not able to open his eyes or speak during that time, he clearly communicated by squeezing our hands when

Journey to the Father

we needed a response. The family surrounded him daily at the hospital and eventually we took turns staying with him through the night. It was now my turn, and I was trembling. Evening came, the family had left, and I stood alone in the doorway of Dad's hospital room. I was 7 all over again. Fear gripped my heart.

About that time, my sister Pat showed up. She'd returned from the parking lot where she had planned to leave with the others. "Becky", she began, "I just realized how difficult this must be for you. I'd like to pray for you." Pat and I had shared a room during my younger fear-filled years. Dad was not the only one who lost sleep on account of me! Her insight in that moment and the prayer that followed is a gift I'll treasure forever.

After tearfully hugging Pat goodbye, she left, and I slowly made my way over to Dad's bed. I put my hand in his. "Dad," I said trembling, "I'm scared." Dad couldn't open his eyes, but he knew it was me. Unable to speak and too weak to move, he made a tremendous effort to communicate. He managed to bring my hand to his heart, turn his head slightly in my direction, and move his mouth. Though no words formed, I knew he was praying for me and reminding me of what the Bible says, *"Perfect love drives out fear."* I snuggled up next to him in the bed like I had done numerous times as a child, sensing the love of God do its perfecting work. Who but God could deliver us from fear by walking us through what we fear most? *"Even though I walk through the valley of the shadow of death, I will fear no evil, for you are with me."* —Psalm 23:4.

The family arrived early the next morning. It was Sunday. Pat entered the room and expressed her sense that this would be Dad's "graduation day," for this was how Dad always referred to the day God would take him home. It seemed fitting to us that it was the Lord's day. God allowed us to be with him that night for his "graduation." Love was present - fear was not. Thank You, Jesus! Thank You, Lord, for giving me a Dad who demonstrated Your love so profoundly. Thank You for being a Father that loves us perfectly.

> *"There is no fear in love.
> But perfect love
> drives out fear."*
>
> *—1 Jn. 4:18*

That last night of Denver's life was a turning point for Becky. As she spent a last night with her dying father, his words of biblical comfort came back to her. Understanding the truth of I John 4:18 reveals that there is a power greater than fear: love, perfect love. The original Greek word for "perfect" is *téleios*, which is used to describe a maturity that comes as a result of going through the necessary stages to reach a goal. "Perfect" love is a full-grown and complete love. Mature, *téleios*, love is like a pirate's telescope which extends one stage at a time until it can function at full-strength. Our love matures as we grow through the stages of our faith. We do not snap our fingers and arrive there in a moment; in fact it is an ongoing journey of discovery. As long as fear remains *in* us, there remains *for* us a greater revelation of the love of God.

I John 4:18 clearly states the remedy and reason for fear. The expectation of punishment is the *reason* for our fear. The remedy is God's perfect love being perfected in us. As God's children, we no longer need to fear punishment because Jesus took upon Himself the consequences we deserve for our sin. Because of Him, we are no longer objects of wrath, but subjects of mercy. Our dread has been replaced with the joyful anticipation of a gift - His perfect love. In Him we are safe, free from all harm, and have no more reason to fear! With these thoughts in mind, read this powerful Scripture once again. Just as Denver reminded Becky of these words many years ago as she faced her fears, they are God's words of truth and comfort to us today.

> "There is no fear in love. But perfect love drives out fear, because fear has to do with punishment. The one who fears is not made perfect in love." —I John 4:18

Our fear was dealt a deathblow at the cross. Understanding and personally appropriating the love of God is our path to a life without fear. Though it may visit from time to time, it no longer defines us. Because the Sprit of God lives in us, we are not held captive by where our minds take us, whether back to painful memories or forward to imagined worse case scenarios. We must remember what we have been given in Christ. The Apostle Paul encouraged his young protégé, Timothy, about this often. He wrote to him, *"For God has not given us a spirit of fear, but of power and of love and of a sound mind."* II Timothy 1:7 (NKJV)

As the Father's children, we need no longer allow fears or phobias to torment us. We don't have to wait until heaven to enjoy this freedom of soul; God wants us to live free now. Through the knowledge of God's Word and the illumination of the Holy Spirit, let your love become mature, "perfect" (*téleios*).

Some say hell (torment) is an empty room with a full-length mirror displaying the image of what we could have become if we'd fearlessly taken the invitations offered to us in life. If this is true then perhaps heaven is a light-filled city inhabited by once imperfect people living in a constant state of awe at the wondrous privilege they had serving God's eternal purposes on earth.

As Jesus told His disciples about His soon departure, He comforted them by saying, *"Peace I leave with you; my peace I give you. I do not give to you as the world gives. Do not let your hearts be troubled and do not be afraid."* John 14:27. As our awareness of God's love grows, our fears diminish and His Spirit-borne peace fills our life. Not a natural peace with earthly origins but the peace of Jesus – *"My peace I give you."* It is a peace that transcends our circumstances and carries us through life, and through death.

As Becky curled up on that hospital bed with Denver that night, she received the perfect love of her heavenly Father; a love that drives out fear. Her faith was tied into a higher truth than the imminent death of her father. She was comforted because she was able to see what was truly precious from heaven's perspective. ." Psalm 116:15 declares, *"Precious in the sight of the LORD is the death of his faithful servants."*

Get into the Story:

1. What would you define as your greatest fear? How have you faced it head on with God's help?

2. Saint John of the Cross wrote, *"O, night that joined the Lover to the beloved one!"* How has God used seasons of night to bring you closer to His love?

   _____
   _____
   _____
   _____
   _____
   _____
   _____
   _____

3. How can you practically begin to live out the truth of I John 1:7 *"For God has not given us a spirit of fear, but of power and of love and of a sound mind."*?

   _____
   _____
   _____
   _____
   _____
   _____
   _____
   _____

17: Father's Love – *"Perfect Love Drives Out Fear"*

18

Father's Favor

> "Sing to God, sing in praise of his name,
> extol him who rides on the clouds;
> rejoice before him—his name is the Lord.
> A father to the fatherless, a defender of widows,
> is God in his holy dwelling." —Psalm 68:4-5

Our loving Heavenly Father knew that many children would lose or grow up without their earthly father, and that many women would be left without a husband. The fatherless and widows were two of the most vulnerable groups of people in biblical history, and God made an astounding promise to both in the above passage: He will be a "father to the fatherless and a defender of widows." Think of it - He who is high in His holy dwelling and "rides on the clouds" shows His unique favor upon those who have lost husband and father. The world might not see them, but they are never hidden from Him.

This truth is powerfully illustrated in the story of Hagar and Ishmael recorded for us in Genesis chapter 16. Hagar was the Egyptian maidservant of Abram's wife Sarai, and Ishmael is Hagar's son by Abram. Sarai is barren. Hagar ends up despising Sarai. When Sarai jealously responds with harsh mistreatment of Hagar, Hagar takes Ishmael and flees for her life. Alone, afraid, and without any hope of a future, the angel of the Lord finds this mother and orphan near a spring in the desert and delivers God's redemptive plan to Hagar. Hagar responds to this miraculous encounter in Genesis 16:13: *"She gave this name to the Lord who spoke to her: 'You are the God who sees me,' for she said, 'I have now seen the One who sees me.'"* Hope for the widow and fatherless today is found in this same revelation. He is the God who sees me.

The father and husband role in the early Jewish culture was one of protection and provision. Faithful to his wife, he was the cohesive hub for his family. He saw to the moral, vocational, and spiritual instruction of his children, and provided for their financial needs. If the husband were to die, his wife and children would be left quite vulnerable and potentially destitute.

We catch a glimpse of this social dilemma in the life of Ruth and her mother-in-law, Naomi. In the midst of a national famine, these women were left in dire circumstances. *"Now Elimelek, Naomi's husband, died, and she was left with her two sons. They married Moabite women, one named Orpah and the other Ruth. After they had lived there about ten years, both Mahlon and Kilion also died, and Naomi was left without her two sons and her husband."* Ruth 1:3-5. Who could imagine that this desperate situation was actually a divine set up? A loving Heavenly Father was at work behind the scene throughout Ruth's redemptive story. He would ultimately rescue and redeem these vulnerable women.

While the enemy seeks to take advantage of the vulnerable, God steps in to extend His favor to them. In the case of the widow and fatherless, He personally assumes the role of husband and father. We can be assured that when God steps into this role, He does so with loving care. His favor is

18: Father's Favor – *"A Diamond from Heaven"*

demonstrated as he meets the largest and most obvious needs, and tends to the smallest and most hidden desires. Often concealed and many times undetected, to the grateful recipient, his actions display His favor like kisses of grace and winks from heaven.

> *"As a father has compassion on his children, so the Lord has compassion on those who fear him"* —Psalm 103:13

—"A Diamond from Heaven"—

Losing Dad was painful. Winter had come and gone, and for my Minnesota family, spring couldn't arrive early enough. The warm breezes seemed to melt and move our frozen grief, and each new bud and bloom signifying life brought us comfort and renewed hope.

When spring was almost upon us, the diamond in my wedding ring went missing. I noticed it one night after a church picnic as I sat down at our kitchen table to write a letter. Some of the prongs had bent and a few of the tips were missing altogether. The empty prongs reminded me of the precious life we'd recently lost.

A thorough search was made, but we did not find the missing diamond. Though this produced a sickening knot in my stomach, losing dad had put real loss in perspective. In comparison, a missing diamond was inconsequential. I put the ring, void of its stone, on a shelf.

I didn't share this experience with anyone, but our immediate family and a close friend who called me the next day. At the conclusion of our conversation, when she asked how she could pray for me, I shared my story, and requested prayer that it might be found. Though the diamond I lost was never found, God provided another one in a most unusual way.

A few weeks after the diamond had been lost Sonny came home for lunch and approached me with a smile and a question, "Are you ready to be blessed?" He asked me to close my eyes then placed something very small in my hand. You guessed it...a diamond. A lady from church had come into his office and told him, "I feel like God wants Becky to have this." Sonny and I embraced as we celebrated this gift. Over his shoulder, my eyes fell on a picture of my Dad and me that was hanging on our refrigerator. Tears began to flow as I immediately sensed God tenderly speaking, "I know your dad is gone, but I am here, and I will take care of you." It was a fatherly gesture from God that I will never forget. In that moment I was reminded of His awareness of, and care for, every detail in our lives. He truly is a "father to the fatherless." (Psalm 68:5)

18: Father's Favor – "A Diamond from Heaven"

The Rest of the Story:

A few days after receiving this diamond, which fit perfectly in my ring's setting, I sat down to write a note expressing my thanks to the woman through which this gift had come. It was then I recalled the first time I had met her. She was visiting our church for the first time and came to me for prayer after the service. Not accustomed to the personal touch of the Holy Spirit, she was moved by the prayer He had given me for her. I had prayed along the lines of a picture God had impressed on my mind of her…as a diamond! Just as a diamond goes through tremendous heat and "pain" in order to show it's true brilliance, so God had seen and had purpose in the pain she had been through. He intended to heal her, allowing her to display His splendor — His brilliance, like a beautiful diamond.

I always wear my wedding ring. It is a constant reminder of the precious marriage covenant Sonny and I share. Now it also reminds me of God's unique favor.

He is a Father to the fatherless!

As Christians, we are part of God's family by "the Spirit of adoption." Perhaps we can better grasp what the Spirit of adoption *is*, by understanding what it *isn't*. Romans 8:15-16 reads, *"For you did not receive the spirit of slavery to fall back into fear, but you have received the Spirit of adoption as sons, by whom we cry, 'Abba! Father!' The Spirit himself bears witness with our spirit that we are children of God."*

The kind of relationship God desires with us is the kind of relationship He offers us by His Spirit. If He had desired us to be His slaves, He would have given us a spirit of slavery. But this is not the Spirit we have received from Him. He has given us the Spirit of adoption because He wants us to be His sons and daughters. He did not intend for us to live in bondage *to* fear, but in freedom *from* fear, knowing we are loved by Him. As His children, we are never abandoned, alone or unheard. On the contrary, we are invited to cry out, "Abba Father," confident of His presence, love and care.

We will always struggle with the spirit of slavery and fear if we have not fully understood the Spirit of adoption by faith. Some authors identify this contrary spirit as an "orphan spirit." Those with an orphan mentality may try to find their value and identity in people's approval, or in what they own or achieve. Others may be controlling and argumentative as they fight for a place of significance in their world. An individual under an orphan spirit may be a Christian and attend a great church, but never feel a sense of belonging. They falsely project onto others their own sense of rejection. I (Becky) was visiting a lady one time who struggled with a deep root of rejection in her life. While we were talking in her yard, an apple fell off of a tree onto the roof of a shed in the back of her property. I saw it happen, she didn't. I was shocked when she said in disgust, "those neighbors are throwing apples at me again." She felt rejected; therefore she perceived rejection in most of her relationships. That's a spirit of slavery!

An orphan spirit cannot be cast out, but is displaced when the truth of our sonship with the Father is understood. The Spirit of adoption informs us that we are loved, chosen, and under God's care. He will provide for us, protect us and use our lives for His glory. Ephesians 1:5 says, *"In love he predestined us for adoption to sonship through Jesus Christ, in accordance with his pleasure and will."* We were not haphazardly chosen or simply tolerated by our Father, but rather adopted according to the *"pleasure of His will!"* The powerful image of adoption speaks to both our vulnerable state and our Father's loving choice of us. Our adoption was a spiritual transaction secured through the atoning work of Christ Jesus. For when we are brought into God's family, we are given all the rights and privileges of His own children. Galatians 4:6-7 further expands on our status, *"Because you are his sons, God sent the Spirit of his Son into our hearts, the Spirit who calls out, "Abba, Father." So you are no longer a slave, but God's child; and since you are his child, God has made you also an heir."*

18: Father's Favor – *"A Diamond from Heaven"*

There are no slaves in God's household, only sons and daughters. Understanding and receiving the Spirit of adoption is vital if we are going to walk in the fullness of our salvation. Both the passage in Romans 8 and Galatians 4 tell us that this privileged status comes to us by the sweet ministry of the Holy Spirit. The life and revelation of the Spirit allows us to call Almighty God, "Abba, Father." We are no longer slaves, but His adopted children and heirs of all the wealth of His house!

> *"Yet to all who did receive him, to those who believed in his name, he gave the right to become children of God"* —John 1:12

Get into the Story:

1. Are you fatherless? If so, how have you seen God step in to be your Father?

2. What is more real to you presently as you relate to God: an "orphan spirit" or a "Spirit of adoption?" (Reread the above descriptions of each).

_____
_____
_____
_____
_____
_____
_____
_____

3. Do you see yourself more as a 'slave' in God's household or a 'child' of His? Why is this?

_____
_____
_____
_____
_____
_____
_____
_____

18: Father's Favor – *"A Diamond from Heaven"*

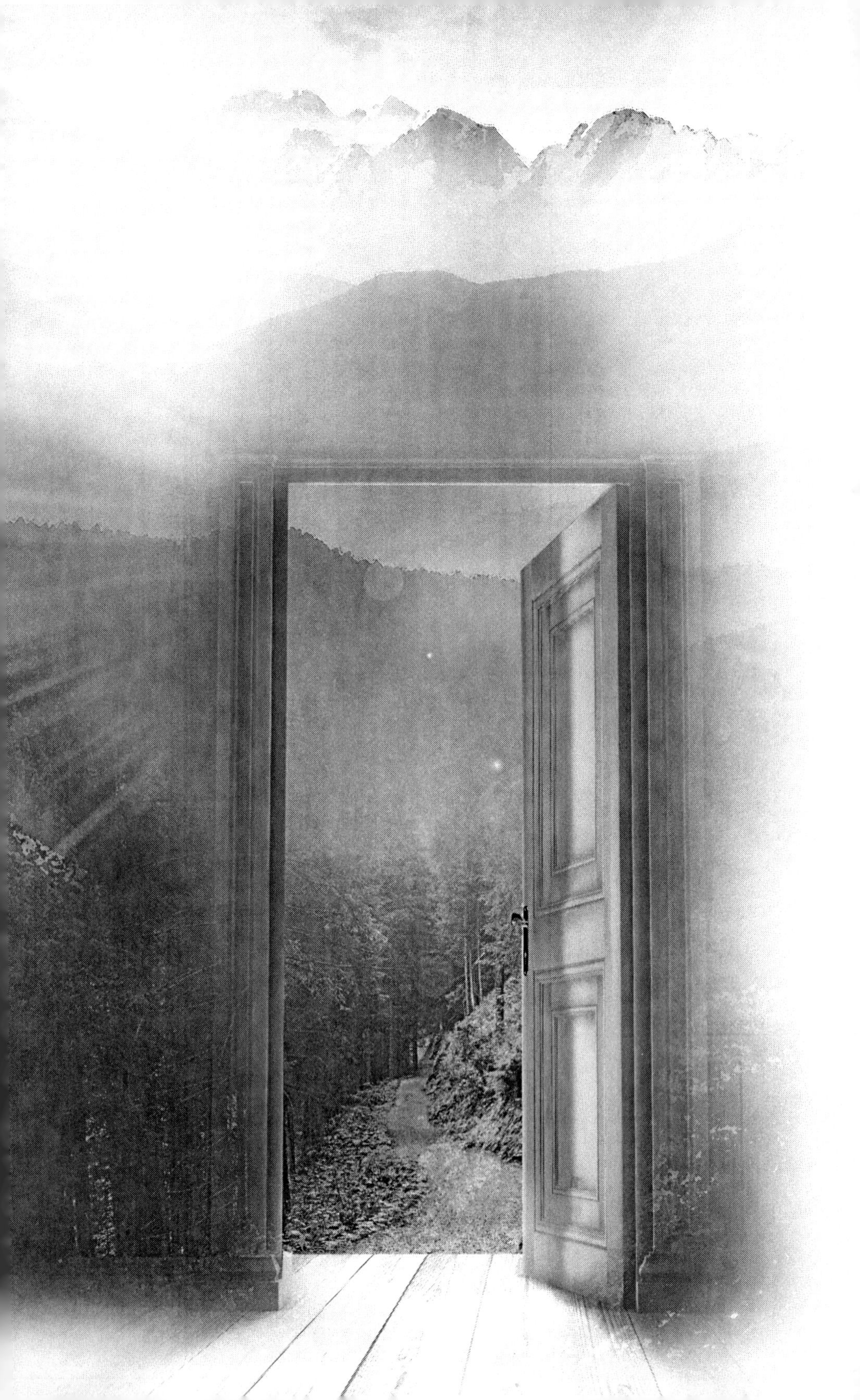

19

Healing Your Father Wound

All this talk of God being our very special Heavenly Father may leave us with a gnawing in the pit of our stomach. If our relationship with our earthly father is distant or has been damaged, we may find it hard to receive this revelation of the Creator as our personal, intimate, and loving Father.

A young woman attended church as an act of desperation. Broken relationships and deep, self-inflicted wounds had devastated her life. But, when the pastor explained the Gospel, her heart was stirred and at the end of the service she went forward to receive Christ's forgiveness. There at the altar, she was met by the pastor who asked her to repeat after him a prayer for salvation. He began, "Dear Father in heaven..." He paused to allow the young woman to repeat after him. There was nothing but silence. He asked her, "What's wrong?" Trembling and with eyes brimming with tears, the woman said, "I can't call God my Father; it's too frightening for me." That exchange opened up an awareness of a significant father wound that woman had carried for many years. The pastor went on to minister both to her need of salvation, and her need of healing, forgiveness, and restoration. The correlation between our natural father image and that of our Heavenly Father is significant and often subtly affects our lives. Like an operating system would for a computer, it runs in the background acting as the framework upon which we build our relationship with God.

Tracing Your Father Wound

The term "father wound" is used by clergy, counselors, and mental health professionals to identify the origin of emotional and behavioral issues arising from the damaging words, actions or inactions of our father. Negative imprints can be made by the extreme ill treatment of fathers such as physical, mental, emotional, and sexual abuse or abandonment. Even more mild actions, such as veiled rejection or harsh words spoken in anger can affect a child. By God's design, the father/child relationship is significant and powerful. We see a glimpse of this in the phrase, *"The glory of children is their fathers."* Proverbs 17:6b (ESV). How our earthly fathers relate to us certainly influences us for good or ill.

Experiencing a father wound of some kind is nearly inescapable. A father who is present, loving, and supportive is still imperfect and sometimes relates to his children in ways that could be perceived as hurtful. Father wounds from otherwise good fathers were very likely unintentional, but our childish minds perceived particular events in a deeply hurtful way. In this case, the saying is true: perception is reality. Seemingly insignificant childhood interactions can revisit us in adulthood, showing us they played a key role in forming our inner world. Some father wounds are the result of a father's struggle with his own interior issues. If we were unable to understand his stresses, we are prone to misinterpret his aloofness or bad moods as rejection. Some people have no memory of an overt wounding experience with their father, but his absence, distance, unwillingness to communicate, or lack of affection conveyed a lack of value toward them. It may not be obvious, but a father wound, at least to some degree, has affected most of us.

> *"When a father's love is withheld, a child will struggle with issues ranging from shyness and insecurity to a profound and crippling shame over his or her very existence."* —Dr. James Bryan Smith

The father wound can deeply and significantly influence how we relate to our spouse, our friends, our children, and our Heavenly Father. Some things that we consider to be an aspect of our personality can actually be attributed to a father wound. For example, some individuals may be insecure, shy, or fearful. Conversely, others may become controlling and dictatorial and will use people for their own agenda or convey a relational harshness. Having been hurt by their father, perhaps they made an inner vow to never be vulnerable again. Father wounds manifest in many different ways. For someone who could never measure up to their belittling father, it might manifest as overachievement, an unhealthy drive to succeed, or the need to always win. If a child's father was overly permissive and unwilling to discipline, they may grow up with an entitlement mentality and a disregard for rules. A child who didn't receive physical affection or words of affirmation from their father may end up searching for it in all the wrong places. This may lead to a confusion of their sexual identity, immorality, or intimacy issues. A father's misuse of authority will likely breed rebellion and distrust in his children for all authority.

Johns Hopkins Medical School commissioned a multi-year study of 1,337 medical doctors who graduated from their university. The study searched for a common causation for four distinct diseases: hypertension, coronary heart disease, malignant tumors, mental illness as well as suicide. The one factor all these had in common in the graduates they studied was a lack of closeness to one's parents, especially the father. The study found that those with a disconnected relationship with their father were more likely to have elevated stress in life, resulting in a weakened immune system.

Questions to Consider

We have found that considering the following two questions is a meaningful and helpful exercise.

1) What is the most *affirming* thing your father ever said or did to you? Do your best to enter into the event and identify how it made you feel.

2) What is the most *disaffirming* thing in your life that your father ever said or did? Like the first question, go back to that experience and to all the emotions and feelings connected to it.

Now, consider how these experiences inform how you relate to God as your Heavenly Father. It is common to find deep and powerful emotions lying just under the surface as these memories are recalled. These emotions arise from more than mere nostalgia; they are tied to the very significant role that God intended the father / child relationship to play in our lives. It is truly significant and often the lens through which we see our Heavenly Father.

A Path Toward Healing Your Father Wound

The following steps will be helpful for anyone regardless of the intensity of their father wound. Take the time to prayerfully work through the process below giving the Holy Spirit open access to the hidden places of your heart.

1. Identify and admit the nature of your father wound.

You may find the two questions in the above exercise helpful for this step, or consider making a list of the hurtful experiences that come to mind. This is not about bashing or blaming your dad, but is more about you and your internal connection to those experiences.

> "Search me, God, and know my heart; test me and know my anxious thoughts. See if there is any offensive way in me, and lead me in the way everlasting."
> —Psalm 139:23-24

2. Allow yourself to feel the pain and the effect of each father wound.

Many of the Psalms depict the raw emotion of David as he wrestled through the real pain of life. Don't make the mistake of minimizing what you felt at the time; it is not unspiritual to feel. Give words to the feelings and emotions that these wounds produced. Grieve over the pain.

> *"In your anger do not sin: Do not let the sun go down while you are still angry, and do not give the devil a foothold."* —Ephesians 4:26-27

3. Take time to objectively consider the inner life of your father, which may have contributed to his hurtful words and actions.

As children, we are not likely to take into consideration that our parents may be living out of their own baggage. The very hurt, rejection, and anger they have experienced bleeds into how they parent. This does not dismiss the wrongs we experienced, but it helps us, now as adults, to see that our dads were imperfect, flawed, but doing the best they could. They were likely bringing their own brokenness into parenting. Ask God to show you your dad through His eyes.

> *"For he knows how we are formed, he remembers that we are dust."*
> —Psalm 103:14

> *"We all stumble in many ways. Anyone who is never at fault in what they say is perfect, able to keep their whole body in check."* —James 3:2

4. Based on how Christ has forgiven you, now choose to forgive your father of the wrongs he knowingly or unknowingly committed against you.

This step may be the most difficult, but it is the most critical one. Remember that forgiveness is a decision, not a feeling. Forgiveness does not mean that we diminish the event, but that we release our father to God. Holding resentment is like taking poison and expecting your offender to get sick. Speak your specific forgiveness aloud to God. Forgiveness doesn't remove the memory, but it lessens the pain of the memory. Whenever you sense a twinge of pain again, forgive again.

> *"Bear with each other and forgive one another if any of you has a grievance against someone. Forgive as the Lord forgave you. And over all these virtues put on love, which binds them all together in perfect unity."* —Colossians 3:13-14

5. Ask your Heavenly Father to move into the places you have forgiven and to reorient, if necessary, your relationship with Him.

Any lies you have believed must be dislodged by the truth of God's Word. The relationship patterns established with our earthly father often transfer to our relationship with our Heavenly Father. Identifying these patterns takes the enlightenment of the Holy Spirit. We must realize that He is the only perfect Father; let His love and truth flow into the places once inhabited by your father wound.

> *"Do not conform to the pattern of this world, but be transformed by the renewing of your mind. Then you will be able to test and approve what God's will is—his good, pleasing and perfect will."* —Romans 12:2

6. Repent of any "inner vows" you made as a result of your father wound.

In the pain of our father wound, we may make inner vows that affect the entire course of our lives. The Bible speaks of the infectious power of a "bitter root" if we allow it to take hold in our heart. When we say, "I will never let someone close to me like that again", or "When I'm a parent, I will never act this way", we are making inner vows. These often unconscious vows are like tender nerves. If touched, we react with an over-the-top response inappropriate to the immediate offense.

> *"Make every effort to live in peace with everyone and to be holy; without holiness no one will see the Lord. See to it that no one falls short of the grace of God and that no bitter root grows up to cause trouble and defile many."* —Hebrews 12:14-15

7. If possible, seek reconciliation with your father.

Obviously, if your father is no longer living, this step is impossible. If he is too relationally toxic, this step should be considered with the help of a counselor. You may consider writing him a letter and rather than mailing it, releasing it to God.

You may reason, "Hey, he was the one in the wrong. He should be the one initiating reconciliation." Meaningful reconciliation is only possible after you do your necessary heart work of forgiveness. Your father may not offer any apology for his offenses and you have to be okay with that. Jesus calls us to be peacemakers, pure in heart and motive.

> *"Therefore, if you are offering your gift at the altar and there remember that your brother or sister has something against you, leave your gift there in front of the altar. First go and be reconciled to them; then come and offer your gift."* —Matthew 5:23-24

After working through these steps, you will discover that living free of your father wound is a *decision* followed by a *process*. Some of your relational patterns may take months or years to reorient to God's Word. Ask the Holy Spirit to make you aware of when you are thinking or acting out of an old father wound pattern and then reaffirm your commitment to walk in wholeness. Your faithful Father will pour out His grace and comfort not only to you, but also through you.

> *"Praise be to the God and Father of our Lord Jesus Christ, the Father of compassion and the God of all comfort, who comforts us in all our troubles, so that we can comfort those in any trouble with the comfort we ourselves receive from God."* —1 Corinthians 1:3-4

19: Healing Your Father Wound

Your Heritage is Not Your Legacy

Receiving a godly heritage is a blessing, but what if all that was passed on to you spiritually was "the sins of your fathers"? Does that leave you less than blessed, or worse yet, cursed? The answer is a resounding no! 2 Corinthians 5:17 tells us, " *Therefore, if anyone is in Christ, the new creation has come: The old has gone, the new is here!* The most amazing thing to us about the godly heritage Sonny and I received, is that we each had a parent (Becky's dad and Sonny's mom) who were first generation Christians. Neither of their father's came to know Christ until late in life.

Denver's dad was a hard-working coal miner, a man of good moral character, and provided for his family, but was rather rigid in how he related to his children. Denver could not recall one affirming word or affectionate touch from his dad. Denver didn't have memories of his dad as a believer, but rejoiced to learn he had received Christ before his death at age 85.

Sonny's mom, Juliette Misar, grew up with an alcoholic and mostly absent dad. Her mom was left, near destitute, with the overwhelming task of trying to raise six kids, born over the span of 9 years. Juliette received Christ at 16 years of age when invited by a friend to a church youth group. Her journey to the Father's heart began with no concept of what it meant to have a dad who loved her. She was astounded when she first stumbled across Psalm 68:5, which says that God is *"a Father to the fatherless."* This discovery greatly impacted her and she set out, as if on a great treasure hunt, to explore its claims. In the early stages of her Christian walk, she may not have always understood how to move toward Him, but His movement toward her was not met with hesitation. She had not seen her dad for many years, but prayed fervently that God would help her find him before he died. She had something she desperately wanted to tell him. Quite miraculously, she finally found herself face to face with her dad after thirty years. "Dad," she said, "I know God brought us together. I asked Him for the opportunity to tell you that you don't have to be burdened about your inability to father me. God has been a good Father in your absence. God has forgiven me and loves me, so I can forgive and love you!" Mercifully, her dad, though still a very broken man, did surrender to the love of the Heavenly Father and became a child of God before he died.

> *"One generation commends your works to another; they tell of your mighty acts."* —Psalm 145:4

Denis Rainey the founder of Family Life Ministries once said, "The heritage you receive is not as important as the legacy you will leave." Certainly, the generations that lived before you influenced what you believe about God, yourself, and the world you live in. However, God's grace can overcome the negative things from your past and free you to pass on a godly legacy. You are the bridge between past and future generations. The Lord wants you to be intentional and strategic about leaving a godly legacy that lasts for generations to come.

A journey to the Father's heart is one of continual discovery. Where we are today is not where we were yesterday and will not be where we are tomorrow as we grow in the Father's love. With the help of the Holy Spirit, we will grow ever more confident in God's disposition toward us. We can rest in His love, based not on our own merit or goodness, but on the gift of God's spiritual adoption. This adoption brought us into God's family and was the primary objective of Christ coming to earth. Galatians 4:4-6 tells us, *"But when the set time had fully come, God sent his Son, born of a woman, born under the law, to redeem those under the law, that we might receive adoption to sonship. Because you are his sons, God sent the Spirit of his Son into our hearts, the Spirit who calls out, 'Abba, Father.'"*

> *"Adoption is a family idea, conceived in terms of love, and viewing God as father. In adoption, God takes us into his family and fellowship—he establishes us as his children and heirs. Closeness, affection and generosity are the heart of the relationship."* —J.I. Packer, *Knowing God*

19: Healing Your Father Wound

It is our prayer that these simple stories have provided a light for your journey to the Father's heart. May each step you take be met with the awareness of your Father's delighted gaze. May your journey be so observed by others that it compels them to joyfully draw near as well.

Appendix A

A Mighty Oak has Fallen in the Woods Today

A Tribute to Pastor Denver Jones, September 5, 2004 by R. Sonny Misar

A Mighty Oak has fallen in the woods today.

It grew straight, strong and true
> among the other trees in God's forest.

Under the Light of the nurturing Son, it sent roots down
> deep into the hidden aquifers of living water.

Towering tall over the green forest canopy,
> it enjoyed the perspective of God's vast timberland.

A Mighty Oak has fallen in the woods today.

Children ran to play, dance and sing under its branches;
> with joy they roped a swing to its strength and carved *"I Love You"* into its gnarly bark skin.

The Mighty Oak always was glad to provide shade for the weary of soul

Without judgment, many were renewed under the embrace of its boughs.

A Mighty Oak has fallen in the woods today.

Through years of storms and winds of adversity
> it stood fast with faith in the One Who plants all things.

Reckless woodsmen once threatened the tree's massive trunk;
> they left their scars, but never brought the Mighty Oak down.

A Mighty Oak has fallen in the woods today.

Appendix A

With the soft winds of summer, one could hear singing among its
    leaves.

In the autumn its brilliant colors would paint a magical glow on
    the dark forest floor.

With branches raised to heaven, higher - ever higher, the Mighty
    Oak would lift praise and adoration to its Creator.

A Mighty Oak has fallen in the woods today.

And what shall we say?

We will look with amazement and we will cry for a time.

We will always remember this Mighty Oak and remember him in
    our living.

For, his inspiration calls us to praise and faithfulness
    – to love and fruitfulness.

Indeed, the soil of our life is richer, for...

A Mighty Oak has fallen in the woods today.

Appendix B

"Because of you, Dad"

Written by Becky to her father, Denver Jones, in 1984 when she was 20 years old

Because of You, Dad...
  I am able to understand the love of my Heavenly Father.

You are trustworthy
  and I feel totally confident placing my life in the Father's hands.

You are reassuring
  and I am not ashamed to let my imperfections show before my Father.

You are a comforter
  and I can share my hurts with the Father.

You are full of compassion and do not hold back love from me
  and I am able to express my need of love to the Father.

You are pleased when I tell you, "I love you,"
  and so is my Heavenly Father. I can easily express my love to Him.

You love me even when I fail you,
  and through that, I understand the unconditional love of the Father.

You are a provider
  and with confidence I express my needs to the Father.

You are strong
  and nothing is too heavy for my father to carry. I give Him my burdens.

Appendix B

You make me feel secure
    and when I am afraid I go to the Father.

You are wise
    and I look to the Father
    to explain things I don't
    understand.

You encourage me
    and I share my achievements with the Father.

You listen
    and so I realize my Heavenly Father also listens.

I understand that I can go to my Heavenly Father any time with anything
    and He'll always be there,
    ready and willing to respond
    because
    He loves me.

I understand this because of you, Dad.
    I thank you and love you
    with all of my heart.

Becky

Appendix C

A Father's Love Letter

My Child,

You may not know me, but I know everything about you (Ps 139:1). I know when you sit down and when you rise up (Ps 139:2). I am familiar with all your ways (Ps 139:3)—even the very hairs on your head are numbered (Matt 10:29–31).

You were made in my image (Gen 1:27). In me you live and move and have your being, for you are my offspring (Acts 17:28). I knew you even before you were conceived (Jer. 1:4–5). I chose you when I planned creation (Eph. 1:11–12). You were not a mistake, for all your days are written in my book (Ps 139:15–16). I determined the exact time of your birth and where you would live (Acts 17:26). You are fearfully and wonderfully made (Ps 139:14). I knit you together in your mother's womb (Ps 139:13), and brought you forth on the day you were born (Ps 71:6).

I have been misrepresented by those who don't know me (John 8:41–44). I am not distant and angry, but am the complete expression of love (1 John 4:16). And it is my desire to lavish my love on you (1 John 3:1), simply because you are my child and I am your Father (1 John 3:1). I offer you more than your earthly father ever could (Matt 7:11), for I am the perfect Father (Matt 5:48). Every good gift that you receive comes from my hand (James 1:17), for I am your provider and I meet all your needs (Matt 6:31–33).

My plan for your future has always been filled with hope (Jer. 29:11), because I love you with an everlasting love (Jer. 31:3). My thoughts toward you are as countless as the sand on the seashore (Ps 139:17–18), and I rejoice over you with singing (Zeph. 3:17). I will never stop doing good to you (Jer. 32:40), for you are my treasured possession (Ex 19:5).

I desire to establish you with all my heart and all my soul (Jer. 32:41), and I want to show you great and marvelous things (Jer. 33:3). If you seek me with all your heart, you will find me (Deut. 4:29); delight in me and I will give you the desires of your heart (Ps 37:4), for it is I who gave you those desires (Phil 2:13).

Appendix C

I am able to do more for you than you could possibly imagine (Eph. 3:20), for I am your greatest encourager (2 Thess. 2:16-17). I am also the Father who comforts you in all your troubles (2 Cor. 1:3-4). When you are brokenhearted, I am close to you (Ps 34:18); as a shepherd carries a lamb, I have carried you close to my heart (Isa 40:11). One day I will wipe away every tear from your eyes, and I will take away all the pain you have suffered on this earth (Rev 21:3-4).

I am your Father, and I love you even as I love my son, Jesus (John 17:23). In him, my love for you is revealed (John 17:26). He is the exact representation of my being (Heb. 1:3). He came to demonstrate that I am for you, not against you (Rom 8:31), and to tell you that I am not counting your sins against you (2 Cor. 5:18-19). Jesus died so that you and I could be reconciled (2 Cor. 5:18-19). His death was the ultimate expression of my love for you (1 John 4:10): I gave up everything I loved that I might gain your love (Rom 8:31-32).

If you receive the gift of my son, Jesus, you receive me (1 John 2:23), and nothing will ever separate you from my love again (Rom 8:38-39). Come home and I'll throw the biggest party heaven has ever seen (Luke 15:7). I have always been Father and will always be Father (Eph. 3:14-15). My question is: will you be my child (John 1:12-13)? I am waiting for you (Luke 15:11-32).

Love,

Your Dad
Almighty God

Father's Love Letter used by permission Father Heart Communications ©1999 FathersLoveLetter.com

Appendix D

Attributes of Your Heavenly Father

1. Creator - One who creates us in his image, with freedom to choose whether to respond to his love.

'In him we live and move and have our being... for we are indeed his offspring' (Acts 17:28).

'Oh Lord, thou art our Father; we are the clay, and thou art our potter; we are all the work of thy hand' (Is. 64:8).

2. Provider - One who loves to provide for our physical, emotional, mental and spiritual needs.

'If you then, who are evil, know how to give good gifts to your children, how much more will your Father who is in heaven give good gifts to those who ask him!' (Mt. 7:11).

3. Friend and Counselor - One who longs to have intimate friendship with us and to share wise counsel and instruction with us.

'Thou art the friend of my youth' (Jer. 3:4).

'And his name will be called Wonderful Counselor, Mighty God, Everlasting Father, Prince of Peace' (Is. 9:6).

'Thou dost guide me with thy counsel' (Ps. 73:24).

4. Corrector - One who lovingly corrects and disciplines us.

'My son, do not regard lightly the discipline of the Lord... for the Lord disciplines him whom he loves, and chastises every son whom he receives... If you are left without discipline... then you are illegitimate children and not sons. For the moment all discipline seems painful rather than pleasant; later it yields the peaceful fruit of righteousness to those who have been trained by it' (Heb. 12:5-6,8,11).

Appendix D

5. Redeemer - One who forgives his children's faults and brings good out of their failures and weaknesses; one who brings us back from being lost.

'The Lord is merciful and gracious, slow to anger and abounding in steadfast love. As far as the east is from the west, so far does he remove our transgressions from us. As a father pities his children, so the Lord pities those who fear him' (Ps103:8, 12-13).

6. Comforter - One who cares for us and comforts us in times of need.

'Blessed be the God and Father of our Lord Jesus Christ, the Father of mercies and God of all comfort, who comforts us in all our affliction' (2Cor. 1:3).

7. Defender and Deliverer - One who loves to protect, defend and deliver his children.

'He who dwells in the shelter of the Most High, who abides in the shadow of the Almighty, will say to the Lord, "My refuge and my fortress; my God, in whom I trust". For he will deliver you.' (Psalm 91:1-3).

8. Father - One who wants to free us from all false gods so that he can be a Father to us.

'And I will be a father to you, and you shall be my sons and daughters says the Lord Almighty' (2 Cor. 6:18).

9. Father of the Fatherless - One who cares for the homeless and the widow.

'Father of the fatherless and protector of widows is God in his holy habitation. God gives the desolate a home to dwell in' (Ps 68:5-6).

10. Father of Love - One who reveals himself to us and reconciles us to himself through Jesus Christ.

'For the Father himself loves you, because you have loved me and have believed that I came from the Father' (Jn. 16:27).

Journey to the Father

There are many other terms in the Bible used to describe the character of our Father God. Listed below are a few of those terms and Scripture references you may want to refer to, as you meditate on the character of our wonderful God. He is:

Patient	Ps. 78:35-39
Considerate	Jn. 2:1-11; 19:25-27
Holy	Jn. 2:13-22
Discerning	Jn. 2:23-25
Compassionate	Lk. 19:1-10
Sensitive	Lk. 8:40-48
Caring	Mt. 9:35-38
Tender	Jn. 12:1-8
Gracious	Jn. 4:7-27
Forgiving	Jn. 8:1-11
Just	Deut. 32:4-5
Loving and Kind	Ex. 34:6-7
Merciful	Lam. 3:23; Lk. 23:29-43
Thoughtful	Lk. 18:15-17
Generous	Mt. 14:13-21; 15:30-38
Powerful	Mt. 17:14-21
Wise	Mt. 17:24-27
Mighty	Mk. 4:35-41
Loving	Lk. 6:27-36

Reprinted with permission from: The Father Heart of God by Floyd McClung 1992; pages 44-46

Credits:

Chapter 1

John Ortberg, *Praying with Power: The Lord's Prayer* (Grand Rapids: Zondervan, 2008), page 19

J. I. Packer, *Knowing God*, (Downers Grove, IL: Inter Varsity Press, 1973), page 181

Chapter 2

Billy Graham, *Hope for the Troubled Heart*, (Nashville, TN: Thomas Nelson, 1991)

C.S. Lewis, *Mere Christianity*, (1952; Harper Collins: 2001) Page 132

Henri Nouwen, Life of the Beloved, (New York, NY: The Crossroad Publishing Company, 1992)

John R.W. Stott, *The Epistles of John* (Tyndale New Testament Commentaries; Eerdmans, 1964), page 49, citing St. Jerome's commentary on Galatians 6)

Chapter 3

Brene' Brown, *Daring Greatly*, (Avery; Reprint edition, April 7, 2015)

Martin Luther, *On Christian Liberty*, (Minneapolis, MN, Fortress Press, 2003)

James Strong, *Strongs Exhaustive Concordance*, (Hendrickson Publishing, 2009), Hebrew #1523

Jack Frost, *Spiritual Slavery to Spiritual Sonship*, (Destiny Image Publishers; November 1, 2006)

Brenan Manning, *The Ragamuffin Gospel*, (Multnomah, June 28, 2005)

Chapter 4

Dr. James Dobson, Bringing Up Boys, (Tyndale Momentum, 2001) page 99

Ann Voskamp, *One Thousand Gifts* (Grand Rapids, MI, Zondervan, 2011)

John Eldredge, *Captivating: Unveiling the Mystery of a Woman's Soul*, (Thomas Nelson Publishers 2011) Page 140

Chapter 5

Bill Hybels, *The Power of a Whisper*, (Grand Rapids, MI, Zondervan, June 24, 2012)

Irenaeus, *Against Heresies*, 4. 34. 5-7

C. S. Lewis, *Mere Christianity*, (HarperCollins Publishers, 2009)

Chapter 6

Philip Yancey, *What's so Amazing about Grace*, (Harper Collins Publishers)

Harvey Turner, *Friend of Sinners*, (Lucid Books, July 28, 2016), page 125

Chapter 7

Abraham Wright, *A Puritan Golden Treasury*, compiled by I.D.E. Thomas (Edinburgh, The Banner of Truth Trust, 1977)

C. S. Lewis, *The Problem of Pain*, (HarperOne; Revised ed. edition, April 28, 2015)

Chapter 8

C. S. Lewis, *The Collected Letters of C.S. Lewis, Volume III*, (HarperCollins Publishers, 2009)

Watchman Nee, *The Normal Christian Life*, (Tyndale House Publishers, Inc.; Reprinted edition, November 4, 1977)

Chapter 9

Amy Carmichael, *Beauty for Ashes*, (Banner of Truth, reprint, January 30, 2015)

James Hudson Taylor quotation: Warren Wiersbe, *Wycliffe Handbook of Preaching & Preachers*, (Moody Press; 1984)

Chapter 10

C. S. Lewis, *A Grief Observed*, (Harper One, February 2001)

Tim Keller, *Walking with God through Pain and Suffering*, (Penguin Books; Reprint edition, August 4, 2015)

Alexander MacLaren quotation, *Forty Thousand Quotations*, Charles Noel Douglas, (New York, N.Y., Blue Ribbon Books, 1940)

Chapter 11

D.A. Carson, *How Long, O Lord?*, (Baker Publishing Group September 2006)

Brian Zahnd citation, (Charisma Magazine, *"How to encourage yourself in the Lord"* 9/23/2013)

Chapter 12

Andrew T. Lincoln, *Word Biblical Commentary Vol. 42, Ephesians*, (Thomas Nelson; November 6, 1990)

Chapter 13

John R. W. Stott, *Tyndale New Testament Commentaries, The Letters of John* (Grand Rapids: Eerdmans Publishing Co., 1996), page 188

Bill Hybels, *Too Busy Not to Pray* (Downers Grove, IL, InterVarsity Press, 2008)

B. M. Palmer, Theology of Prayer, (Sprinkle Publications, 1980)

Chapter 14

Francis Schaeffer, *Pollution and the Death of Man*, (Carol Stream, IL, Tyndale House Publishers, 1970)

J.D. Greear, *Gospel: Recovering the Power that Made Christianity Revolutionary*, (B&H Books; October 1, 2011)

Chapter 15

Brennan Manning, *The Furious Longing of God*, (Colorado Springs, CO, David C. Cook; March 1, 2009)

Chapter 17

Max Lucado, *Live Loved: Experiencing God's Presence in Everyday Life* (Nashville, TN, Thomas Nelson)

Saint John of the Cross, *The Dark Night of the Soul*; Chorus, Public Domain

Chapter 19

Dr. James Bryan Smith, *Rich Mullins: An Arrow Pointing to Heaven*, (B&H Publishing Group, LifeWay, 2002)

Johns Hopkins Medical School study: Claudia Wallis, *"Stress: Can We Cope?"* (Time magazine, June 6, 1983), 48-54.

Also available by R. Sonny Misar

Journey Series

I invite you to come with me on a journey; a pilgrimage of sorts. This journey is not over land and sea, but is through the passages of the human soul. Our discoveries will not be of gold and lost cities, but of our own identity in Christ. This is a unique journey because it is directed by the hand of God. In fact, the word pilgrimage means a journey to a sacred place. That sacred place is where we find the mysterious mingling of both divine intention and human will. This spiritual journey enables us to discover ourselves, our God and our place in His greater purpose on earth.

Journey to Authenticity
Discovering Your Spiritual Identity through the Seasons of Life
R. Sonny Misar

Also Available in Spanish

Purchase your copy at Amazon.com or wherever books are sold.
For discount orders of 10 or more, email JourneyMinistriesLLC@gmail.com

What Readers are Saying About "Journey to Authenticity"

"At a time when many are finding it difficult to 'finish the race' due to weariness and confusion, Pastor Sonny Misar has given us a practical road map to assist us in fulfilling our destiny. **Journey to Authenticity** will help you discover where you are at on the journey and what adjustments need to be made to hit the mark. ...A must read for all believers!"

— *Pastor Larry Borud, Apostolic Team Member, U.S.A.*

"As we journey through life we encounter different stages or seasons and it is God's plan that we would grow spiritually through each of them – that we would gain a greater understanding of who we are in Christ. It has been my experience that not every season has felt like a growth stage, but in *Journey to Authenticity,* Sonny Misar, in such a personal and practical way, helps us to see how God is shaping our lives in every season. You'll be encouraged as you read and you'll definitely want to dig deeper into God's plan for your amazing journey."

— *Pastor Dale Hewitt, Perth, Australia*

Journey Ministries, *Serving those who Serve, Ministering to those who Minister, and Equipping those who Equip.*

Blessed are those whose strength is in you, whose hearts are set on pilgrimage. They go from strength to strength, till each appears before God in Zion.
—Psalm 84: 5, 7

To plan a speaking engagement or discuss a training seminar for your church or ministry, contact Pastor Sonny & Becky Misar - see below.

Would you prayerfully consider standing with Sonny & Becky Misar of Journey Ministries in prayer and financial partnership? Your involvement will allow us to be sent out to assist pastors, missionaries and church leaders around the globe.

Become a Monthly Support Partner!

ONLINE: Give safely and easily at www.RadiantWinona.com
- Choose the "Give" tab. Click on "Give Online".
- Click on "Please Select".
- Scroll down to find "Journey Ministries – Sonny and Becky Misar."
- Enter your personal giving preferences and information.

BY MAIL: Make checks payable to **Radiant Church** – in memo: **Journey Ministries**. Mail to the address below.
Journey Ministries, 930 W. Burns Valley Rd., Winona, MN 55987
www.JourneyMinistriesLLC.com   Email: JourneyMinistriesLLC@gmail.com   Phone: (507) 450-9176

Journey MINISTRIES